PRAISE FOR
THE LIZARD IN YOUR MIND'S EYE

For anyone who thinks spiritualism is all crystal balls and cliché, this is a refreshing corrective – written with clarity, intelligence, and warmth. Whether you're a believer, a sceptic, or simply open to the possibility of more, *The Lizard in Your Mind's Eye* is a quietly captivating read.
— *Harriet Nobel, Editor, Exeter Living Magazine*

The Lizard in Your Mind's Eye is a beautifully woven journey of spirit, intuition, and inner knowing. Blending the mystical with the everyday, it gently reminds us to listen more closely to the world around us, and to what's already within. Honest, tender, and quietly powerful.
— *Rebecca Jenkin, Somatic and Psychic Guide*

I loved this book – Fran's powerful storytelling resonated with me long after I'd finished reading it. The way she weaves lived experience with spiritual insight is both comforting, in that it brings things into an embodied perspective you can feel into, and thought-provoking, in the way that it makes you then reflect. Fran brings compassion, curiosity, and a deep reverence for intuition and nature to her writing, that for me represented a beautiful reminder to trust your inner knowing.

— *Jenny Guyat, Personal Transformation and Career Coach*

Whether you've ever wondered why we're here, are already open-minded about what may lie 'behind the veil' or have already experienced some psychic phenomena, you need to read this book! Fran's lucid collection of short stories and interviews with working mediums and healers reveals a rich tapestry of spiritual activity, most of it designed to help and support us as we navigate our way through this journey that we call life.

— *Claire Wright, Communications Professional*

Sceptical of all things in and around the Psychic World. *The Lizard in Your Mind's Eye* changed my thinking, and awareness of these not so hidden messages we often hear but ignore. If you don't believe in such experiences, read this book and I guarantee you'll think differently the next time something unexplained happens to you.

— *Chris Marren, ICF Professional Certified Coach*

An interesting and thought-provoking story about spiritualism and the direction your life could take if you could hear messages from the other side. A very good read.

— *Helen Hardy, Human Resources Professional*

A beautifully written, thought-provoking story which will open your eyes to the 'other side'.

— *Paula LeBlanc, Healthcare Professional*

The Lizard in Your Mind's Eye

A story about how the spirit world guides us

Fran McElhone

Copyright © Fran McElhone 2025. All rights reserved.

This book or any portion thereof may not be reproduced or used in any manner whatsoever without the express written permission of the publisher except for the use of brief quotations in a book review.

Strenuous attempts have been made to credit all copyrighted materials used in this book. All such materials and trademarks, which are referenced in this book, are the full property of their respective copyright owners. Every effort has been made to obtain copyright permission for material quoted in this book. Any omissions will be rectified in future editions.

Cover image by: Slobodan Vukovic / WolfBell
Book design by: SWATT Books Ltd

Printed in the United Kingdom
First Printing, 2025

ISBN: 978-1-0681731-0-3 (Paperback)
ISBN: 978-1-0681731-1-0 (eBook)

Fran McElhone
Budleigh Salterton, Devon

For Woody, Jessica and Myles

Light will always overcome darkness.

CONTENTS

CHAPTER 1	Rainbow Lake	9
CHAPTER 2	The Statue	14
CHAPTER 3	Brother Joseph	22
CHAPTER 4	Morning Cloud	30
CHAPTER 5	All Paths to the Same God	40
CHAPTER 6	Florence	55
CHAPTER 7	The Celestial Book	62
CHAPTER 8	Humans v Mother Nature	78
CHAPTER 9	The Caravan	87
CHAPTER 10	Simon	94
CHAPTER 11	Journey West	99
CHAPTER 12	Marnie	105
CHAPTER 13	Small Signs	116
CHAPTER 14	Orbs	128
CHAPTER 15	Nibaa	133
CHAPTER 16	Readings	144
CHAPTER 17	Belle	173
CHAPTER 18	New Life Next Party	191
	Friends' Experiences	193
	Glossary	212
	Recommended reading	217
	Acknowledgements	218
	Author's note	219
	About the Author	220

CHAPTER 1

RAINBOW LAKE

Driving overland across Canada, you gain a sense of the enormity of the world. The distance between Canada's most westerly point to its most easterly point is longer, by around 1,000 miles, than the width of the Atlantic Ocean. Canada's interior is predominantly plains. Thousands of miles of wilderness.

If you didn't have a map, you could probably hazard a guess at where you were in the country by the topography and geology of your surroundings. When you hit Alberta, giant rocks and snowy peaks pierce the surface of the Earth, bursting up with the drama of an opera singer's opening note. Glacial lakes spill a striking turquoise over a craggy landscape, proliferated with evergreens. And, Nova Scotia in the east, is a rolling quilt of deciduous trees, which turn the land a russet hue in October, pocked by thousands of lakes.

All my life I felt like I was born in the wrong country. I yearned for mountains and forests, to be a speck in the wilderness, which is why I chose to move to Canada for a couple of years after university. Canada felt like home to me. It felt like you could escape anything there.

And then years later, I found myself returning to do exactly that. Escape.

Our destination was Peace River in Alberta. Our 5,304-kilometre journey across the country was uneventful. We spent our hours on the road sharing stories and musing about what we might find when we arrived in town. Would we be the first there? And, then what? We knew all we had to do was listen. And trust.

Given the vastness of the land, at every pitstop we would enquire about the next gas station, motel or convenience store, which could be many many miles away, so we weren't caught short. The people we met on our way were going about their lives as normal, albeit the topic of conversation was dominated by the unprecedented cyberattack that had closed all the airports on the west coast of the North American continent.

CBC's news coverage escorted us west and we heard Western governments bickering about which autocracy was behind it. At this point, other than North American aviation being in chaos, there were no other indications being communicated via the state news broadcaster about the impending apparent doom we were escaping from, according to our spirit guides. We all had plenty of what-on-earth-are-we-doing moments, but our guides assured us we were doing the right thing.

I felt so guilty when we met friendly souls along the way, passing the time of day with them. I wanted to tell them to come and join us. But I also knew that there was a ninety-nine per cent chance they'd just laugh if we'd said anything other than, 'We're on a road trip to Vancouver Island', instead trying to explain that, actually, we were one step ahead of the rest of the world and were undertaking this journey to avoid the possibly imminent Armageddon.

After six days on the road, it was mid-afternoon when myself, my thirteen-year-old son Sonny, and our new friend Marnie, arrived in Peace River. A small town with a population of around 8,000, the main industries there were forestry, agriculture, and oil and gas extraction. It was another hot day, around twenty-eight degrees. White clouds morphed into various shapes in a pure blue sky. Pedestrians milled about. There were only a few cars, all SUVs, buzzing around. Life was ticking along. But we felt an uneasy energy.

We spotted a bar-restaurant downtown with a sunny veranda on a quiet side street, so parked up and had the pick of the array of metal tables outside. It was a normal working day for the locals. No sooner had we plonked ourselves down, a waitress in her twenties with the sunny demeaner shared by all North American waitresses, appeared, brandishing menus and a smile, welcoming us with a cheery, 'Hey, guys, how's it going for you today?'

Upon hearing that two of us were from England and the other from Maritime Canada, the conversation played out predictably about the whys and wherefores of our trip to Canada's northwest. 'We're taking a trip to Vancouver Island,' we said. 'We're just taking a small detour to take in the sights up here.'

We didn't know if the locals would be convinced by our cover story, but she didn't appear fazed and, as we ordered, we quizzed her about the local area. We didn't know whereabouts in the area of Peace River we were supposed to be heading – in the town or on its outskirts. But nothing in what she, the daughter of the longtime owners of the bar, said, gave any hints or clues about our supposed destination; the surrounding area was more wilderness.

After finding a hotel, for the rest of the afternoon we wandered around the town like tourists looking for a gift shop that didn't exist, making casual chit-chat with shop owners who, unbeknown to them, were part of our research as we tried to gather as many nuggets of information as we could to work out our next move.

Maybe we *were* the first ones here?

Later on, we found another bar to have dinner. We sat down and Sonny was drawn to the rainbow illustration on the menus, which we thought nothing of, before ordering grilled chicken and a round of Caesars (virgin for Sonny). The next morning over breakfast, as we were chatting, Marnie and I realised we'd been given the same message as we'd fallen asleep that night, and again when we woke (when you're relaxed and your mind is in a more lucid state, you're more receptive to receiving intel from spirit): our destination wasn't Peace River, it was Rainbow Lake, 431km to the north, hence Sonny picking up on the imagery too. Our messages were from Black Claw, a former chief of the Dene Tha' First Nations people, who occupied three reserves in the area.

Spirituality underpins the culture of indigenous North Americans – First Nations Canadians and Native Americans. Core beliefs include the existence of a Creator or Master Spirit, the immortality of the soul and an afterlife; beliefs which are shared with major world religions. What is *not* typical of other, institutionalised religions, however, are the beliefs that the natural and supernatural are intertwined, and that we all have guardian spirits. Objects and elements of the Earth, both living and non-living, have an individual spirit that is part of the greater soul of the universe, therefore the spirit of the land is revered.

Nature, and all life is sacred. Trees, for example, represent more than just a source of life; their spirits emanate permanence and longevity. And spirit animals are gifts from the Creator, to guide us.

Just like Pearl, my dear late friend whose prophecy had got us here, Marnie also had a Native American guide.

CHAPTER 2
THE STATUE

My hands were turning a deep shade of ochre, coated in a wet gritty paste the rich colour of the sandstone cliffs that rose up behind me and into the sky from the pebbly beach I was digging at with them. My fingers had become numb with the cold.

'Where the hell is it?' I berated myself, while rolling my eyes at the comedy of the escapade. A fine mist of drizzle was showering from an opaque, pale grey sky and I was becoming damper and damper. I started flinging pebbles to all sides of me. I must have looked so weird to anyone else on the beach. If there was anyone there, I wasn't aware, I was so engrossed in my self-appointed task. I spun around, changing location half a dozen times, each time clawing at the slippery pebbles with my bare hands.

'I swear it was here,' I said under my breath, 'I only buried it this morning.' Strands of hair were sticking to my face now and I began to feel fatigued by the absurdity of it all. Then, finally, I spotted it. A tuft of feathers, the headdress, was sprouting out of a fist-sized, ebony-hued, wooden head. I grabbed at it, yanking at it, throwing it down beside the recently decapitated, spindly wooden body of the African tribesman I'd unearthed a few minutes ago several inches beneath the surface of the beach, a couple of metres away.

I swung round towards the shoreline where the waves were pounding the pebbles. The rhythmic hushing sound of the stones being dragged back and forth by the strength of the tide became louder, filling the air. This dramatic soundscape to my current predicament was apt. Hurriedly, before they became too wet to use for a fire, I began scouting for straggly pieces of driftwood and the odd bit of seaweed plus a few larger logs, stripped naked of their bark during their journeys out at sea.

I spotted a shallow dip in the stones filled with a bed of ash and pulled out the scrunched-up newspaper I'd stuffed in my jacket pockets and added it to the remnants of what was a recent, late summer barbecue, scattering the kindling on top.

Kneeling down on wet pebbles, I lit the corners of the paper which disappeared as I blew into the flames. Sheltering the fledgling fire from the drizzle with my arms, I took a few more breaths and watched the flames multiply and the damp wood fizz as it reluctantly caught fire.

I placed the willowy wooden headless body on the burning twigs, before lobbing the head on top. It sizzled instantly as the headdress became engulfed with fire. Ignoring the damp, which was now seeping through my shorts, I stared at it as it burned, watching it disintegrate and become indistinguishable from the ash of the barbecue coals underneath.

I sat there and waited until it disappeared.

The statue had been a rare gift to myself, my first frivolous buy for as long as I could remember. At the end of each month there was little left over after rent, bills, and saving for a deposit on a house that, despite all the years of scrimping and saving was still a far-off prospect; as our savings increased, so did property prices. So a purchase of this nature was pretty indulgent for me.

At first, I didn't regret the purchase. And when I strode away from the tiny shop, an emporium of ethnic artefacts from around the world, my hand clasped around the chieftain's neck, I comprehended the innate desire within people to buy stuff for themselves, the appeal of materialism. Having nice stuff does make you feel happy, I mused. This sentiment didn't run deep, mind. The only possessions I owned when I reached my forties (other than clothes and furniture) were plants, a few books, and a handful of sentimental items.

At this time, years before Sonny came along, I lived with Sam, my partner of seven years, husband for two, in a flat on the second floor of what used to be a 1950s' era hotel overlooking the sea in the small twee East Devon town of Budleigh Salterton. When I got the statue home, I fluffed up its headdress and it became pride of place on our mantelpiece.

When my mum next paid us a visit, her reaction fell far short of the admiration I had been hoping for. She said something like, 'Oh. Yes, well... it's OK I suppose.'

'How can you not like it? I love it,' I told her. 'It was made in Africa and imported over. It's authentic African craftsmanship. There's a sense of power to it.'

'I don't know,' she hesitated. 'There's just something I don't think I like about it.'

Not good. My mother had a fairly good sixth sense these days. On the other hand, her dislike for clutter could have been skewing her judgement. From then on, whenever she came over for a cup of tea she'd only give it a glance, accompanied by a contorted grimace. Any more attention would make her recoil. She didn't tell me how much it offended her though, not wanting to upset me. And I, unusually, remained oblivious to its charms.

Sam, meanwhile, who was still only developing his sixth sense, felt a sense of distrust towards it, but, he said, it was 'only a statue' and he knew how much I liked ethnic wares.

But it wasn't long before I started getting a bad feeling about it too, and I started seeing lost souls making their way towards our balcony from out at sea.

A perfect cube from the outside, our building was dystopian ugly. Inside, a lack of sunlight rendered the stairwells and hallways interminably cool. The walls were plain cream and the carpets mud brown; a helpful colour seeing as mud was often clogged in our trainers from weekend hikes, trail runs and bike riding in the surrounding fields and woods.

A slightly claustrophobic lift connected all four storeys plus the basement, which housed the building's foundations and was comprised of myriad breezeblocks and concrete pillars. This is where superfluous items, usually stored in sheds, garages or outhouses (for those with houses), were stored. In our case, it was where we crammed our mountain bikes, surfboards and camping gear.

But despite its façade, tinged with copper due to the dust from the nearby cliffs, the flats inside that faced the sea, like ours, were full of warmth and light. Ours was one of the smallest in the block. Double-glazed doors opening out on to a balcony extended along the entire front wall of the lounge, so when the sun was up, our whole flat was flooded with sunlight. In winter we barely had to switch the heaters on.

Our balcony overlooked a large, seldom used, communal garden. The block, our friends joked, was an 'old people's home'. It was full of mainly retired professionals; some eccentric, others nosy, and some you only knew existed when they passed over.

The garden was an expanse of tantalisingly verdant lawn edged with flowerbeds full of giant plants. A path dissected it, leading to a small wrought-iron gate with a clanky handle, which opened out onto the promenade, beyond which was a twenty-metre-high grassy verge and the beach below. To the right, the promenade morphed into a path that led up and over the clifftops.

There was nothing in the rule book about not using the garden, but we figured it was an unwritten rule, because no one ever did. Apart from Six Toes. This was the name we gave a portly ginger cat which had six toes on each foot and used to make a beeline for us whenever he spotted us. One day, he stopped coming into the garden. I knew he hadn't died; his owners had just moved away.

We stayed there for four years until we found ourselves needing more space and moved to a house elsewhere in the town. The sea and its ever-changing moods never got boring.

It was about a fortnight after I brought the statue home that I started getting a really bad vibe from it. I always tried to make sure I left my desk at the local newspaper, where I worked as a news editor, on time. Sam, on the other hand, was an electrician, so couldn't exactly leave a site, or someone's home, if the power wasn't on, so more often than not I was always home before him.

So, there I was, about five o'clock on a Friday evening. I'd come in, left my shoes and jacket in the hallway, and sat down taking a moment to enjoy the serenity of the view over the sea, when I began to feel a really oppressive energy in the room. I knew exactly where it was coming from. Sam too, when he came home, sensed the same thing.

I met Sam when I was twenty-three. I'd just finished my degree in religious studies and philosophy and was desperate to move to western Canada and live in the mountains and snowboard. I'd always been drawn to the mountains; their wild majestic beauty resonated with me at a soul level. On Earth, for me, they were as far as you could get from reality. They're my spiritual home. In my second decade, I'd only managed to wangle a few days here and there skiing, but I was drawn to winter sports due to the sense of freedom, escapism, empowerment and acute joy they bring. So, in my final year of university, I arranged a work visa and then in the October, packed a few items of clothing into a sixty-five-litre backpack, bid farewell to the UK, and headed 4,620 miles west, by myself for a while.

Sam, five years my senior, grew up in Nova Scotia, Maritime Canada, on the east coast. When he was twenty-three, he swapped this verdant corner of Canada, which turns into a blazing scarlet in autumn and becomes frozen with snow and ice in winter, and headed out west to interior British Columbia to snowboard, where he ended up working in the saw mills.

We both blossomed from economically deprived roots, with a shared love of the outdoors and adventurous sports. Our paths crossed because we both had the exact same idea. Sam had been living in the Coast Mountains village of Whistler, a bubble of non-reality, a valley exuding a hedonistic carefree energy, for four seasons when I moved out there in the early Noughties. We met on my first day there and got together within a couple of weeks. When we had a deep and meaningful conversation about spirituality, we knew our bond was more than just skin deep.

Sam grew up with two older brothers. First on navy bases on the outskirts of Dartmouth, across the harbour from the capital, Halifax, then in Dartmouth's sprawling suburbia where their garden backed onto woods which led to the banks of one of many lakes in the area. Sam was the smallest of the three boys, at 5'8". He was 'pretty' handsome, with a wavy crop of brown hair and a soft nature. His dad was away for the entirety of his childhood with the Canadian Navy. Meanwhile, his gentle-natured mother did the best she could to bring up her three sons while suffering with bipolar disorder. Since he was a dot, Sam had witnessed the whole range of emotions of which the human mind is capable.

The three brothers grew up fending for themselves as their mother was preoccupied with the pendulum of her mental state – high as a kite one minute and bedridden for weeks the next, sucking the life out of her, blocking out the light, robbing energy from her flesh and bones. Too often the cupboards were bare when their dad was away from port and all there was to eat was ketchup sandwiches, and for years in junior high he wore the same school trousers which ended up skimming his ankles. But you would never meet a more loving soul than Sam's mum. Sam maintained that he didn't feel a lack growing up because of the love she gave him. And because he earned money from his paper route from the age of twelve. He enjoyed life and studied hard at school, skateboarding in his free time and going to church with his mum on Sundays. When my visa ran out, Sam left Canada behind to start a life with me back in the UK. Our intention was always to return as soon as possible, but sadly life didn't play out that way.

'We haven't seen Pearl in a few weeks,' I said to him, later that evening. 'Let's go tomorrow.'

We were both keen to consult with her about the statue.

CHAPTER 3

BROTHER JOSEPH

'Come on, Spiro, in you go. And you, Strauss. Come on, Sheriff, you too. Night night,' Pearl said to her three companions before turning in herself.

It only took a limited amount of cajoling to get her cats in their baskets for the night. During her lifetime, Pearl had owned eighteen of them. Not including the strays she used to feed on her doorstep over the years. Every single one of her felines' names began with the letter S, for no particular reason other than it became a tradition after the first two, Saber and Shadid.

Most of Pearl's cats were long-haired, and she'd owned several Persians. All had varying dispositions and characters, including the one that saw off an Alsatian. And every single one of them had won her rosettes, all the colours of the rainbow, a fluttering of which were on display around her compact council bungalow, located up a lane in the tiny village of Axmouth. The rest were stuffed into any available nook or drawer alongside a lifetime of knick-knacks, none of which had sentimental value; she didn't feel that way towards inanimate objects, she just found her collectables nice to look at and they made the place more homely.

Latterly, as Pearl entered her eighth decade, her cats were house cats. She'd tired of them bringing home rodents every other day. 'Poor little things,' she used to say when coming across a not-quite-dead mouse or an almost decapitated sparrow on the carpet. She loved all animals. One of the many reasons I loved her. Regardless that she was three times my age, she was one of my best friends.

The view from her sitting room window consisted only of fields that rose up steeply on the other side of the lane to the height of the clifftops a mile away and were more often than not home to a flock of noisy sheep, their bleats echoing around this emerald valley, theirs the only sound to break the silence.

Pearl was in her seventies when we met her. She was sturdy and strong, topped with a crop of soft white hair, tinted with a little wash-in blond, with knowing, twinkly pale brown eyes. She wore black almost exclusively, her silver rings and wedge of silver bangles, which jangled as she moved, were an extension of her.

Pearl lived alone for almost all her life. She moved to Axmouth upon retiring from her job as a care worker in nearby Seaton, where she'd lived in a rented flat overlooking the sea for the best part of three decades. But despite her longevity in the town, she had never liked it. It had a bad feeling about it, she said.

She used to get visits from the spirits of people who had died at sea. So many of them would come, she said. Sometimes on their own, sometimes in pairs or groups. And sometimes small families. All were victims of the sea, their lungs full of briny liquid at the end, their passing too traumatising for them to find the light. They were lost. Lost souls of the sea. Some had been waiting a century or more to find the light and pass over into peace.

It would surprise Pearl to see their attire, usually in her mind's eye, other times as clear as day standing right there in her living room with her. Sometimes the ladies wore floor length cotton dresses done up to their necks, fringed with lace. But they weren't sopping wet, despite their fate. Most bore the same look on their faces. Most would stare at Pearl with sad eyes. Forlorn. Desperate. Looks of confusion from their perpetual wait in a timeless zone.

When you're psychic, earthbound spirits know this. You emit an energy they can pick up on. More often than not, they make themselves known to you because they want to be noticed, seeking acknowledgment of their trauma. Some know they're dead, others don't. Some want help going over to the Other Side, others don't.

Pearl would spend a lot of time and energy sending lost souls over to the Other Side; soul clearing she called it. Psychopomp. She would close her eyes, as if in meditation, visualise a bright golden white light, and telepathically, or verbally, tell the lost souls to go towards it.

Soul clearing was also an activity of the healing circle she attended in the town each week. Members would take it in turns to host a small gathering of spiritually-minded people with the purpose of channelling positive energy towards those who needed it most, both living and dead; people whose journeys have ended on the earth plane often need healing too. This might be because the time leading up to their passing over was difficult, or if the passing itself was difficult. Besides, healing energy, or just good vibes, are always a nice way to help someone settle in their new home on the Other Side, regardless of their disposition at the time of passing.

It was in Seaton that Pearl took a strong dislike to the sea. It wasn't evil, she would say, just indifferent to the lives it claimed and the adverse impact of its power. It had no contempt, just no compassion, no mercy, either.

Inwardly, she would wince when people expressed how much they loved the sea, how they loved staring wistfully out across the blue void to where it merged with the sky, or how they loved watching the boats return to the harbour. I could tell she didn't share the sentiment when I told her I loved living by the sea. It gave me a sense of space and escapism. But no psychic is the same; we pick up on, and are affected by, different things.

But I felt too that the ocean is untrustworthy, an entity which needs respecting and indulging in with caution. When Pearl moved the half a mile up the Axe Estuary to Axmouth, she had no fond memories of Seaton and felt anything but sentimentality for her previous bluish view.

Nevertheless, Seaton was her home for some thirty years as she worked long, unforgiving shifts at different residential and nursing homes, caring for people with all sorts of joyless afflictions associated with old age and the human body's mortality.

Before settling in Seaton, Pearl had lived a nomadic life. Not through choice, but out of fear for her safety and that of her only daughter, Anne. She never spoke about the man she married, and I never pressed for details in all the years we were friends. All I deduced was that he was an unkind, unpredictable character, so much so that she sacrificed a normal life for her and her daughter to make sure he never found either of them.

Anne was only a year old when Pearl decided she'd had enough. She packed their bags one morning, got on a bus from Derby to somewhere in the Peak District and found herself a job on a farm out in the sticks, looking after the horses. And this was how they lived for the remainder of Anne's childhood.

Living out of bags they could carry on their backs, mum and daughter would move from farm to farm, where Pearl would work from dawn till dusk, housekeeping or with the horses, come wind, rain or shine, to earn enough money to keep them fed and able to move on, if need be, so he could never find them.

An unfortunate consequence of this itinerant lifestyle was Anne's unsettled upbringing, meaning she had to hop from school to school until they moved to Devon and she started secondary school. She did well though and made her mum proud, forging a successful career as an accountant and marrying a pleasant man. But there was a distinct lack of closeness between Anne and her mum for the rest of their lives.

Pearl had always believed in God. She'd been brought up a Christian, but when she became old enough to make her own choices, she shunned church. Like me, she felt that you didn't need a building to connect to divine energy, just close your eyes and tune in. But she did believe Jesus was the son of God, and that it was in His compassionate footsteps that we should strive to follow, not the religious dogma of humans.

But Pearl did not give God or Jesus much thought when, after the umpteenth time of upping sticks, young child in tow, one frozen winter she found herself so hard up she couldn't afford new boots, the ones on her feet letting in the wet and cold through ragged holes.

She had no parents she could turn to. Her father was nice enough but had passed away by then, her mother wasn't. So, Pearl didn't have much to do with her. Years after her death, she came through to Pearl and apologised, sobbing with remorse.

Pearl hadn't always been a medium. Her ability to act as a conduit to the spirit world and communicate with those who had passed over didn't manifest until she was in her mid-forties in the early 1970s. But when the gift manifested, it turned on like a light switch.

One particular bitterly cold winter's evening, Pearl returned to her room after a long day, dog-tired and overwhelmed. She and Anne shared an annex off a 19th century red brick farmhouse owned by a vet, a well-to-do man in his late sixties. Now divorced and his children having flown the nest, he rattled around the house and left the yard duties, care of his five horses and the housekeeping, to Pearl. He loved animals but was a hard man who hid his emotions so well you'd think him incapable of feeling anything.

'Pearl, I'm heading out, and I don't know when I'll be back,' he bellowed from another room that morning, before setting off before 8am. Pearl had been up since 5.30am, tending to his small flock of chickens. Luckily the fox that had previously made off with one of his finest cockerels had not made a return the previous night. 'There's a pheasant in the larder that needs plucking, and don't forget the delivery of hay is arriving this morning,' he continued. 'Oh, and the dogs need a bath today as well, rolled in something by the smell of them, the whole house has a wretched stench.'

It was nearing 10pm when Pearl's day came to an end. She kicked off her boots, clogged with mud, one at a time against the wall. Already the yard was beginning to gleam iridescent with frost that would become a thick ivory crust by morning.

Only able to see by the light of the moon, which was shining like a spotlight in an inky black sky speckled with tiny fairy-light stars, Pearl leant heavily against the wall trying not to lose her balance but was unable to stop herself from stepping onto the frozen steps in her socks while she eased the boots off from each of her feet. Exhaling deeply with fatigue, causing a cloud of steam to billow towards the door, she twisted the cold metal handle, leaning all her weight against it to push it open.

Hanging her heavy woollen coat on the hook on the other side of the door, with the moonlight filtering in through the windows, she didn't bother reaching for the light switch but padded across the floor making her way upstairs to her bedroom, the wooden stairs creaking underneath her. There, she sat down on her bed and cried. She exhaled loud heaving sobs of utter despair and exhaustion, not just from this day, but from many days, over many years.

Her face wet with despair, she became distracted by a bright light that appeared to be coming from outside in the farmyard. Wiping her face dry, Pearl looked up towards the window. The curtains were open and, assuming it was just the owner returning home, the light the beam of his torch, she remained seated on the edge of her bed.

But, instead of making its way elsewhere, like a man with a bright torch inspecting his property before bedtime would have done, the light persisted. Suddenly the light was no longer outside the room, but inside, its rich golden rays as bright as the sun, eclipsing the window frame and obliterating everything else around it.

Pearl's forehead creased with surprise, her eyes squinting in the beam of light, and then, before she had time to react, in the epicentre of the light was the face of the Virgin Mary. The Holy Mother radiated beauty, purity, and benevolence. If it were ever possible for a face to appear as love and kindness, it was her face, at this moment.

And there she remained, just looking at Pearl with a soft but penetrating stare which pierced through her flesh and bones into her soul, smiling and sending love. Pearl felt neither shock nor bewilderment, just peace, and a sense that when you feel totally alone, you're not.

After her experience with Mary, Pearl started hearing Brother Joseph, a short, kindly, 16th century Buckfast Abbey monk we came to feel we knew personally, despite him being so 'far away'. Brother Joseph would remain Pearl's spirit guide for the rest of her life. Despite his last life on Earth being some five hundred years ago, his outlook was timeless. In the beginning, Pearl would hear him in her mind's ear, but soon began to hear him as clearly as if he were standing next to her and talking into her actual ear. Mary had come to Pearl, Brother Joseph told her, to tell her that her life's work as a spiritual healer was about to begin.

Over the next four decades, Pearl would go on to heal – in person and absently – countless people and animals, never once charging a penny.

CHAPTER 4

MORNING CLOUD

One Saturday evening, not long after moving into her Axmouth cottage in the 1980s, Pearl was treated to another vivid and profound spiritual experience.

Pearl's day began like it did every week with housework and a trip to the supermarket. Her good friend Terry, tall, humorous, mild-mannered (you'd never have guessed he'd had a spell inside), and with a long pony tail, would give her a lift to go shopping once a week in return for healing on his back. A work injury some years before had rendered him in almost constant pain. He got by thanks to a combination of Pearl's healing, his therapy dog, Joy, a large, friendly rottweiler (with a full tail – he hated the practice of docking dogs' tails), and smoking the odd spliff.

They would have lunch together at Pearl's bungalow, and then in the afternoon, after his healing, Terry would leave and Pearl would get picked up by the owners of a nearby farm where she went twice a week to give healing to their two mild mannered horses and temperamental pony. Returning home after dark, she'd feed her three cats and open a tin of something for herself.

After tea was when Pearl did her absent healing. Under her armchair she had a shoebox full of dog-eared photos and newspaper cuttings of people who needed healing, collated over months and years. She also had a well-worn notebook containing an ever-growing list of names she'd compiled of people she'd either met, been told about, read about, or seen on TV, who needed healing. Brother Joseph would tell her if they'd got better or had passed on.

This Saturday, after ushering her cats to bed, she padded slowly into her bedroom. Throughout the winter months, a chill stung the air inside her bungalow. The only heater, a portable gas fire, was in the living room. Pearl's shoulders were slightly hunched, bearing the weight of six hard decades, and she rubbed the base of her back which had begun to trouble her more and more recently. She got into bed and pulled layers of blankets up to her neck to keep winter at bay and finally lay down. Unable to drift off to sleep she lay still, listening to the occasional hoots of a nearby owl.

Unaware of how long she'd been lying there, Pearl began to smell the sweet earthiness of wood smoke. Faint at first, it became starker, thicker and more pungent. Warmth infiltrated her cool bedroom. Then she felt her body detach from the solid bed beneath her and float up towards the ceiling. Leaving the heaviness of her human form behind on her bed, a sense of weightlessness defined the next moments. She rose up, and up, and up. And then found herself sitting in a circle of Native American elders.

She was engulfed by warmth and wood smoke and surrounded by the low, melodious humming of a dozen or so men with resplendent feather headdresses. They sat either side of her, cross legged on a coarse woven mat. The intimate circle of chiefs followed the circumference of the impenetrable, curvaceous walls of their wigwam.

And there she sat, for how long she did not know, time's relevance lost, taking her time when it was her turn to draw in a lungful of strong warming smoke from a spindly wooden peace pipe, making its way from chief to chief to Pearl to chief. Song and smoke awoke every sense, a meditative peace taking over, so powerful that she had no desire, or need, to question what was happening to her, not even where she was, or why and how she had come to be there. All she knew was that it was happening, as clear as day.

When Pearl woke up in the morning, the lingering scent of wood smoke still permeated her night clothes.

Among the group had been a chief called Morning Cloud. From that day on he became one of her guards. While we all have spirit guides, the more psychic among us also have guards to fend off interference from less than pure spiritual influences. Given their spirituality, it's no coincidence that many mediums have Native American guides and guards. Once they have returned to spirit, many have generously opted to guide us, in the hope that mankind follows a more compassionate path than the one they were subjected to, and still endure, here on the earth plane.

This, like the visit by the Mother of God, was one of many extraordinary stories Pearl relayed to us as if it were a standard everyday occurrence, in the most non-sensationalist manner. But this was Pearl's way. And, after some initial amusement at the matter-of-fact way in which she spoke about these extraordinary paranormal events, I realised that we all spoke about the spirit world, and seeing, hearing and smelling spirit, in the same understated way. To the experienced psychic, seeing the odd person wander past and then disappear, or hearing the odd sound coming from something with no physical form, is normal.

Pearl would talk to Brother Joseph about anything and everything so had a deep insight into most aspects of life, both spiritual and physical.

Some years after the disappearance of British toddler Madeleine McCann in the Algarve, Portugal, in May, 2007, Pearl contacted the police hoping her message would be passed on to the team overseeing the investigation. Whenever she tuned in and meditated on where the missing girl was, she always got that she was alive and that she had been kidnapped by a woman and a man who were desperate to have a child but couldn't conceive. She heard that she was living with them in a secluded spot, inland, in the western Algarve.

The vision she had was of a house plotted at the end of a track surrounded by a beige arid landscape. She was so convinced, that on her behalf, her eccentric but well-meaning male friend, twenty years her junior, flew to Faro, rented a car and drove around for a week trying to find the girl, who would have been in her teens at that point. We can only assume the police didn't take Pearl seriously because her phone calls were never returned.

I've always thought there was a case for 'psychic spies'.

It was 2009 when Pearl came out with one of her most astonishing prophecies. During a conversation about geopolitics and the war in Afghanistan, which had been under way since the 9/11 terrorist attack in 2001, Pearl said, 'Brother Joseph says the country to watch is Syria. There are going to be awful things happening there.'

I had travelled a fair amount by this point and was engrossed with geopolitics, yet knew nothing of Syria's political background because the country lay on the periphery of major news headlines. So, at the time, when she came out with this, I just thought it really odd that a place that wasn't on the radar of the vast majority, could or would erupt into global consciousness in the way she'd predicted.

Two years later in 2011, the Syrian Civil War broke out. It was a sickening and protracted war over many years, believed to have claimed the lives of over half a million Syrian civilians and displaced millions of its citizens thanks to President Assad, whose murderous actions were bolstered by his equally devilish Russian counterpart, President Putin.

In early 2009, Pearl also predicted that Britain's Liberal Democrat party would 'get in' to government. This was hard to believe given that the Conservatives and Labour were Britain's main parties at the time. But she was right, in a sense. In May 2010, a General Election resulted in a hung parliament, with no party winning an overall majority. The Conservatives clinched the most seats but in order to form a majority government, they needed to form a coalition with another party, either Labour or the Liberal Democrats. They chose the LibDems, unsurprisingly, with their Leader, Nick Clegg, becoming deputy Prime Minister. The Conservative-Liberal Democrat Coalition remained in power until the next election in 2015.

Pearl used to call a spade a spade. She would deliver short, blunt statements as she heard them from Brother Joseph. Nothing was sugar coated. I would always say how grateful I was for her wisdom, and she would retort, 'It's not me, it's Brother Joseph.'

But Brother Joseph wasn't her only source of enlightenment. She was a master of psychometry, a form of extrasensory perception whereby someone can tune in to the energy of absolutely anything, from inanimate objects, plants, countries, continents, insects, animals and humans.

One of the most disheartening things she ever said in the 2000s, but maintained until the day she died in 2013, was that seventy-five per cent of humans, globally, are actually not very nice. Of the remainder, fifteen per cent are 'iffy', so have undesirable traits such as selfishness, or lack compassion, for example, leaving just ten per cent who are genuinely nice. The other sad thing she said was that people could be born horrible. Because, while our bodies may be new, our souls may not be.

But while there were some serious revelations during our hours-long conversations, we also had some fun with Pearl's psychometry prowess. We'd get her to do it on all sorts of things, like the flies buzzing around her bungalow in the summer. Always detestable! And she told us that flowers don't all like each other! For example, if you put carnations and roses in the same vase, the carnations try and kill the roses.

During her psychometry, which would last only a few moments, whenever someone, or something, wasn't very nice, Pearl's face would scrunch up, the corners of her mouth curling downwards, and she would take a sharp intake of breath through her nose. But if someone was pleasant, she would open her eyes, smile, and say, 'very nice', or, 'he's lovely, nothing nasty about him'. We would ask if we wanted more nuance and then she would go back and tune in again to pick up on why, whoever it was, wasn't very nice, for example, and then give us the specifics.

There were times when Pearl was also overcome with emotion. Clairsentients can sense or feel energy. In the case of objects, which resonate the energy of their owners, clairsentients can take on those emotions.

For this reason, I have avoided second-hand stuff throughout my life and got rid of things I may have initially found aesthetically pleasing if I started sensing something not nice about them. The statue is a case in point. I ended up getting rid of a ring I'd picked up from a charity shop as a teenager, many years later. It had a tiny dried flower under a transparent plastic coating. One day, I put it on after many years of it being hidden away in my jewellery box, and my guide told me the original owner was a horrible woman and if I didn't get rid of it, I would start taking on her energy.

But Pearl, while being a medium and clairaudient, clairvoyant, claircognisant and clairsentient, was also very well protected by her guards. They were responsible for an invisible barrier around her, a shield against detrimental, negative energies (while warding off mischievous spirits). But she was so strong a medium, most of the time her energy repelled anything negative around her. So, for her, it was absolutely fine to have a home full of all manner of second-hand trinkets, furnishings and ornaments.

When we asked her, she would happily oblige and do psychometry on her things, one of which was a mustard-hued painting of a vase filled with flowers, set in a dark wooden frame with a stand. Pearl had placed it on the floor in front of the gas fire she never switched on because she couldn't afford to, in her lounge. Within seconds of tuning in, she was overcome with sadness and began to cry. She said the lady who owned it had been very sad and had taken her own life.

We asked Pearl to do psychometry on whole nations too. In the Noughties, England wasn't nice. Canada, was lovely. The US, not nice at all, nor France. New Zealand was lovely. In this case, the psychometry relates to the human inhabitants, collectively, not the land mass. And we'd get her to do it on famous people:

Freddie Mercury, lead singer of Queen, not nice; Michael Jackson, nice, and not guilty, apparently. Princess Diana, lovely. Queen Elizabeth, lovely.

It was Pearl who told me I was a lightworker, a deeply spiritual person who is here to bring about positive change in the world. We were meant to meet because she was my mentor. I used to call her The Oracle!

'Pearl, hi, it's me,' I called out, pushing open her front door. I rubbed my feet hard on the mat inside the tiny porch; she always insisted we didn't have to take our shoes off. Simultaneously, I clasped my other hand around the cold metal door handle which had become loose through years of use, and let myself into Pearl's sitting room. The door made a hushing sound as it opened across the thick rugs Pearl had put down to hide the worn dark blue carpet underneath.

'Oh, hello dear,' she replied from her usual arm chair, where she sat pensively, bangles jangling, stroking her large long-haired tabby, Spiro, who was sprawled across her lap.

'How are you?' I asked, bending down, giving Pearl a peck on the cheek.

'I'm fine, dear.'

'What have you been up to?'

'Oh, the usual, just my healing,' she replied. 'I've added a few to my healing list this last week or so. How are you, dear?'

'I'm fine,' I said. 'But I did want to ask you about something.'

I began to explain about the statue I'd bought and its intangible darkness. When I listened to my guide, I was told to get rid of it, but wanted to check with Pearl that I was hearing correctly.

She listened, head bowed and resting in her hands. She did this when she was listening – to two people.

'Get rid of it,' she said, looking up suddenly. 'It's not good. Not good at all. Hang on, let me do psychometry on it.'

Pearl lowered her head again, closed her eyes and tuned in to the energy of the person who had made the statue. This method enabled her to feel the overarching emotion and intent of whoever it was she was tuning into. And whereas most psychics who have the rare ability to practice psychometry need to be able to touch the person or object in question, Pearl merely had to picture it in her mind's eye. After a few seconds, she took a deep inhale through her nose as she raised her head again, frowning, the corners of her mouth curled downwards.

'It's evil. And it's attracting evil things to it. You need to get it out as soon as possible. Hang on, let me ask Brother Joseph what he thinks.' She fell silent again. 'It's had a spell cast on it,' she said after a brief pause. 'Whoever made it put a spell on it.'

'But why?'

'All he's telling me is that the person behind it was up to no good. A mischief maker.'

'So what should I do? Should I just take it up to the recycling centre? It's only a mile up the road.'

'He's saying not to take it up there – it could end up in someone else's hands,' Pearl replied after a few moments. 'No. He doesn't want you to get in the car with it. The only way you can break the spell is by burning it.'

That evening, when we got home, I put it outside on the balcony for the night. The next day, there was more out there than just the statue. I could see in my mind's eye spirits coming off the sea, amassing outside the building. It was like a beacon.

'What are we going to do with it?' I said to Sam. 'We've both got work today, what would we tell our bosses? Sorry I'm late, I had to dispose of a possessed statue?'

'Well, one of us has to get it out of here,' he replied. 'Before it starts doing any real harm.'

'OK. You stay here,' I said. 'I'll go and bury it on the beach, and then I'll go back later, dig it up and burn it.'

Sam got up, opened the bedroom door and started rummaging through the cupboard in the hallway. After a minute or two, he pulled out his camping hatchet, strode into the living room and grabbed the statue. Sliding the door open to the balcony, he bent down and took the statue, beheading it with one swift swing. Just in case someone was to find it, we figured it would have less influence if it was headless.

After breakfast I took the head and the body to the beach and buried them, separately, a few metres apart. Sam watched me sweep down the path on my mission. When I got back, he told me that a darkness, like dark grey smoke, had been trailing behind me. He said he'd blinked, not believing what he was seeing, but continued to see a pool of dark mist, hovering, shoulder height, billowing upwards, following me to the beach. When I walked back, he said the cloud was gone.

I returned later to dig up the head and torso and burn them. And break the spell.

CHAPTER 5
ALL PATHS TO THE SAME GOD

I WAS ABOUT SIXTEEN WHEN I became convinced of a spirit world, comprehending that we are first and foremost spiritual beings housed in a physical, mortal, form. Intuitively, I'd always believed this. But sixteen was when I knew.

Myself and my brother Robert, two years my senior, were brought up within the framework of Christianity which included the occasional church visit and a bout of Sunday school aged ten followed by Confirmation aged twelve. Like most kids, we went along with what our parents told us. The context for household beliefs being whatever the norm is in your immediate community and society, which in our case, in Devon, UK, was, if anything, Christianity.

But church services didn't resonate with me; while understanding some of the reasons people have for going, like the sense of peace and community they can bring, I never felt I needed church to bring about this connection. And I found reciting centuries-old prayers and singing hymns not just tedious but irrelevant. I thought God would prefer less worship and more action.

I had always felt numinosity in the natural world around me. The woods and the fields were my church. There were certain places where I felt God's presence more than others. One such place was an elevated area of scrubland near where I grew up and then returned to live as an adult. Teeming with bramble bushes, nettles and ferns, and crisscrossed with grassy tracks, it was surrounded by tall evergreens. The space was big enough for a large church and I imagined the trees as stone buttresses stretching towards a high arched ceiling. An open-air church. In nature, you can feel God's arms wrap around you.

At the same time, and what led me to study world religions and philosophy at university, I was fascinated by the various belief systems around the world, how spirituality and faith, religious beliefs, customs, traditions and rituals captivated millions of people, shaped whole cultures, defined land masses and underpinned the political narratives of whole nations, while being so diverse, sometimes colourful, and at times wonderfully wacky.

There were paradoxes aplenty and there was oppressive dogma, but also excitement and joy and a will to do good.

I always felt that there was a God or Master Spirit and Creator who is benevolent and believed that Jesus was the Son of God as per the Trinity, and that he was as compassionate as he was badass, sticking up for those who live on the fringes of society, including those in its underbelly. I liked the connection prayer offered to divine energy, the feeling of being heard, and I was drawn to the essence of selflessness and 'love thy neighbour'.

Unless you're brought up in an oppressive environment where curiosity and free thinking are suppressed, skewing your judgement, there comes a point where your cognitive and emotional development reaches maturity and you start questioning the things you've always been told, and form your own opinions about things that you've learnt, or which have come to your attention. I like to think of it as the blossoming of your personality, which is representative of your soul and the real you, your *higher self*.

Possessing an open-mind and tolerance for the beliefs of others, I recognised the validity of other belief systems that were different to the one in which I'd been raised; that my cultural framework, due to my country of birth and the parents I was born to, wasn't the only one with meaning or truth.

At the heart of the major world religions (bar Buddhism) is the belief in a supreme deity, or god. Each have their own sacred texts and stories and their own fêted humans or prophets, messengers of God. But rather than there being a god per religion, as my comprehension of other belief systems developed, it became clear that all these faiths were simply different paths to the same god. It's tragic, I thought, that we can't agree to disagree, given that the core message of all religions is righteousness.

Believing the contents of a religious text never sat easy with me either. Because, while all religions claim truth in their texts in that they reflect the word of God and are divinely inspired, they are written by humans. And humans are seriously flawed. The trick is discerning the morals from the stories.

Just as I'd felt intuitively, Pearl warned against taking religious doctrine literally and advocated the need to exercise rationale. While the stories told within the sacred texts of many world religions contain messages of how to live lives of love, tolerance and compassion, the themes of retribution, misogyny and homophobia, also feature.

So while religious texts can be regarded as a guide for living that aligns with humans' inherent moral compass – a rationality which is unique to our species giving us a sense of right and wrong – it was common sense that intolerance, discrimination and violence didn't correlate with belief in a benevolent creator.

There are many quizzical declarations in the Bible, which, in my younger years, I would recite during church visits along with the rest of an unquestioning congregation. But there is so much that doesn't make sense. Like, the assertion that *Jesus died to save us from our sins*. How did His death 'save' the rest of mankind? This expression is a human construct. Jesus died for us, yes, but to show us that we have free will: Jesus was God's only son, and yet, facing torture and death, God didn't step in and save him.

I also pondered polytheism, belief or worship of more than one god, and wondered whether there were actually multiple gods and goddesses, manifesting distinct divine attributes or presiding over specific aspects of reality, or whether they were symbolic and represented distinct divine attributes.

Polytheism is typical in Greek, Roman, Egyptian, Norse and Celtic Pagan belief systems, to name a few, dating back way before Christianity, with many gods and goddesses posited. There are earth, wind, fire, water, solar, lunar, fertility and love deities, gods and goddesses for war, healing and beauty. Also, gods of wine and chivalry, and goddesses of cats and music. The list is endless.

Do they really all exist I wondered? I first started contemplating the reality of multiple gods and goddesses upon learning about Hinduism – which is not categorically polytheistic because not all its adherents believe in multiple deities – and had the strong sense that they are all representations of the one and the same God of all religions. Many years later, Pearl explained that all these gods and goddesses are 'human constructs to help us understand God'.

While I never questioned that all of the religious texts held some truths about the divine, be they symbolical, metaphorical or an apparent recounting of reality, it was blatant that common sense and rationality were required to avoid blind dogma, and quite frankly, being fooled.

So, the biggest turn off to religion for me was people – specifically, how people used religion to manipulate others for their own benefit, and the hypocrisy and contradiction among those who believed in a benevolent being while claiming that God has 'chosen' ones. People had institutionalised the essence of the religious texts, placing an emphasis on the authority of people, more so than that of God Himself. For example, the sacrament of Confession in the Catholic faith, whereby priests are believed to have divine authority bestowed upon them to forgive the sins of someone who repents, on behalf of God.

It is fascinating, liberating and perplexing in equal measure that our interpretations of the same texts led to the major world religions encompassing a variety of denominations, schools, sects and branches. It was the extreme views among some of these believers and their animosity towards one another, which put me off religion, as a human construct, even more.

And, because common sense has been ignored in preference for a literal interpretation of the scriptures, I found it absurd that there were religious adherents – who all claim to be the soul bearers of truth – who were unable to comprehend that God would want us to choose the most compassionate and loving stance on matters.

The result being sexual orientation-based discrimination – the first gay marriage to be blessed in the Church in England took place in December 2023; the first time the Church of England formally acknowledged same-sex relationships – homophobia, rejection of contraceptives or medical intervention, and worst of all murder and war. A recent case-in-point being the Russian Orthodox Church's unwavering support for Russian dictator President Putin even while he dropped bombs on innocent people in Ukraine in the 2020s. We can only imagine what God is feeling about all the wars in His name!

It became my enduring belief that humans were perverting the fundamental notion underlying all the world's major faiths that God created us all and we should show kindness and love to one another. And the intolerance of people towards adherents of other faiths was arrogant and contradictory. So later on in life, when people said to me, 'I don't like religion, religion causes wars,' I would reply, 'Does football cause hooliganism? No. People do. Does religion cause war? No. People do.'

Spirituality was what resonated: that there is one God, Great Spirit, divine source energy, it doesn't matter what your favourite label is, neither does it matter what label you give yourself, Christian, Muslim, Hindu, or whatever, because what matters is kindness and compassion. Because, we all come from the same place; every living being has a soul, or spirit, which comes from a spiritual dimension, occupies our physical body, and then returns to the spirit realm when we die.

God and those in spirit work with us and we can communicate with those in spirit; the physical and spiritual dimensions are distinct yet inextricably intertwined. We are spiritual beings, first and foremost, here to learn, remember our divinity and to love, and experience this through embodiment. The body is the antennae to the divine, it's how we bridge the gap between heaven and Earth.

Both mindfulness and meditation are important tools to achieving spiritual awakening. Being mindful, drawing your awareness and consciousness into the present moment – living in the moment – is a state of being conducive to contemplating and appreciating philosophical notions such as impermanence, cause and effect, and gratitude, leading to a more content, less anxious existence. Deeper understanding and appreciation bring us closer to Source, more in touch with our higher selves, and more likely to hear spirit.

To live in the moment, one must willingly free themselves from the past. Putting too much emphasis on the past is counterproductive to spiritual growth. We learn from events in the past, but they no longer matter because they're gone. Done. Over. And there's nothing you can do about them. Reflect, learn and move on. Neither is there any point in contemplating what the future may hold, because how you behave and think now will help determine that. The only way of finding inner peace is to focus on today. Like my paternal grandfather used to say, 'There is no future. The future is now.'

Meditation – calming and quietening the mind – is a method of attaining inner peace. Meditation enables us to tune in and receive messages from spirit too, through visions, drop-in thoughts or a sense of knowing. Often my guide would hold my hands in meditation; I could feel my hands being clenched by pure energy which was so strong it felt like real hands clasped around them.

I'd always struggled with humans and their behaviour towards one another, animals and the planet. And I struggled immensely with the injustices in the world. It was all an affront to the morality

I felt. It followed then, that I didn't feel comfortable with most humans, even being a human. I felt distant and different from my species. Through personal experience and observation I saw humans as inherently flawed, even inherently egotistical. Another reason I naturally disassociated myself with organised religion, seeking a direct connection with pureness and goodness, not one which went via humans or bricks and mortar.

I was young when I started contemplating life's existential and philosophical questions, like the meaning of our lives on Earth, life after death, ethics, and moral dilemmas. I was a teenager when I first heard the term 'philosophy' and realised it encompassed all the questioning thoughts I'd been having as I contemplated the world around me.

It was in my late twenties when I began to feel a closeness to Mary, Mother of God. Queen of Angels. The ultimate goddess! While the Catholic faith repelled me, due to dogma superseding common sense (for example, the opposition to artificial birth control/condoms in African nations rife with HIV and AIDS), and reports of impropriety among its clergy (not exclusive to the Catholic denomination!), coupled with the ostentatious opulence of the Vatican's real estate in Rome, I felt inclined to agree that Mary deserved veneration and an elevated status.

During a particularly difficult time in my life in my mid to late twenties, I decided to ask her for help. I didn't know where else to turn or who else to ask, and, because of Sam's loose upbringing as a Catholic and his penchant for the rosary, I thought about her and felt intuitively that she had the power to help me and that I could receive her help.

So, one evening, sitting on my bed in a suburb of south Bristol, I said the Hail Mary, believing, *feeling*, that she was listening. And, when I finished, I felt a dark veil had been lifted, my acute anxiety had dissipated. Around the same time, my paternal grandmother 'told my mum on me' from the Other Side! She could see the distress I was in and came through to my mum, unannounced, and told her, 'She can't cope'. My mum heard her words out of the blue, while doing housework one morning.

Mary's status contributes to the age-old debate of whether we should use the male pronoun to describe God. While God is formless, so genderless, using gender helps us understand, and relate to a being which is, essentially, beyond our comprehension. For some, labelling the divine 'male' reflects the patriarchal society predominant on Earth. But it makes sense to refer to God as male because He was Jesus's father, while the Virgin Mary was his mother.

My beliefs into adulthood were the result of a mix-and-match approach. My spirituality became a fusion of eastern and western spiritual concepts. For example, I'd always believed in the notion of souls, and heaven being the spirit realm we return to when we die.

I also believed in Karma, a central belief of Indian religions. In essence, Karma is the principle of cause and effect; there are repercussions for our actions. In this way, victims of wrongdoing can take comfort that, ultimately, justice will prevail, if not in this earthly life, then the next. Belief in Samsara, or rebirth, followed. Not in reincarnation exactly, and not human to animal reincarnation, just that our souls come back in different human bodies, numerous times, as we learn and develop spiritually. Brother Joseph confirmed both beliefs to be true.

Why Christianity didn't place more emphasis on the spirit world, despite the assertion that our souls go to the Kingdom of

Heaven when our physical bodies perish, had long confused me. Jesus was a spiritualist. He heard voices in the desert (Mark 1:3) and infamously rose from the dead following his death on the cross, revealing his spirit to Mary Magdalen. When it came to religious fundamentalists, I wondered if they shunned spirituality because spiritualism poses a challenge to religious dogma; raising more questions than can be answered with a textbook. Spiritualism transcends religious dogma.

Up until I was sixteen years old, I'd had the odd paranormal encounter, but, like many people who experience something similar, I hadn't particularly identified them as such. They were all too vague for me to be sure, like seeing the shadow of a person flit by out of the corner of my eye, or smelling a very strong scent in the room, like wood smoke from an open fire, tobacco, or a lady's perfume.

There were times I'd heard noises, strange sounds that couldn't be pinpointed to a particular thing, and noises that would be audible on the left side one moment and then over to the right, the next. Other times, my encounters were more energetic, feeling a strong sense that someone was present in the room. I could pinpoint where they were exactly, to my left, sitting beside me, behind me, sometimes above me, or over in the corner of the room several feet away.

As a teenager, I was sure my cat who died when I was eleven often visited. I could sense his presence. One time I felt him nestle in the crook of my knees against my calves as I lay on my side in bed. Other times I would catch a glimpse of his shadow scampering across the room.

Naturally, I believed all living creatures had souls and were sentient beings, each and every one created by God and each and every one having a place in heaven when they died. All the cats I've owned since have come to snuggle up to me on my bed at one time or another after they passed over. And I always know which one it is paying me a visit.

During my degree, which involved deep contemplation and understanding of various belief systems and philosophy of religion, I decided definitively that I couldn't possibly just call myself a Christian anymore; there was too much I questioned and too much in other belief systems that resonated. Nevertheless, I always used to tick the box next to Christianity on formal documents requesting your religious belief. There wasn't enough room to explain!

But my paranormal experiences weren't the sort of thing I talked about or shared with others at that time of my life, just in case people thought I was weird. As I became older, I thought non-believers were the weird ones, and I stopped caring about whether people thought I was weird or not! And besides, the paranormal always makes for an interesting conversation.

As the years went by my experiences became less vague and I realised that everything I'd seen, heard, smelt and felt – which didn't feel like they were of this earth (because they weren't) – were not my imagination, but as real as anything completely tangible in physical form.

It wasn't until I was much older that I learnt about a group of people who are soulless. They're not human but reptilian, masquerading as humans. They want to dominate Earth and control people for their own amusement and gain. An energetic war between them, the non-humans and humans, has been going on for hundreds of years, with the non-humans wanting the human collective consciousness to stop evolving, and to be capped. Every two hundred years or so, they manage to reset our collective consciousness.

We're coming up to that two-hundred-year mark again. But this time is pivotal because we're on the cusp of breaking this cycle. The more our consciousness rises, the more light we hold in our bodies and the more we remember our true selves, our soul gifts and our multidimensional personalities, and the more connected to the divine we become. And, the stronger we are, the more we're able to defeat malevolence.

As the vibrations speed up in our energetic war, the result will be very tumultuous occurrences on Earth.

One of the most fascinating and divisive issues facing scientists and religious adherents, is the relationship between science and religiosity. Are they distinct, as in they serve to answer different questions and can therefore work alongside one another? Or, paradoxically, are they distinct as in they serve to answer the same questions and are therefore in competition?

The liberating thing about spiritualism is that this conundrum doesn't exist, as both science and religious discourse can sit alongside one another. If you don't take the scriptures written by men literally, but as metaphors, science and religion are entirely compatible. A complete misnomer is trying to explain spiritual phenomena by the methods of science. For example, take Creationism, the belief that God created the world in seven days as per Genesis, Chapter One of the Old Testament. There can be harmony with the Theory of Evolution as first told by scientist Charles Darwin in the Origin of Species if the story is taken symbolically; 'survival of the fittest' is how evolution played out and God is the answer as to why it played out.

Ultimately, the chances of the Big Bang occurring and producing a planet with the optimum conditions for life to flourish, felt like scientific proof that the origin of the planet was *caused* by a far greater entity than could ever be conceived by the human mind.

The principle of Occam's razor helps out here. It states that simpler explanations are more probable than complex ones. So, when it comes to the creation of the world, how can it be that out of an infinitesimally small chance of existing, we do? Human nature demands more of an explanation than mere chance. The alternative, simpler, argument is that we exist *because* of God.

Really, atheism shouldn't really make sense to scientists. Ultimately, faith is at the epicentre of religion and spirituality. But scientifically, there are very good reasons to believe more exists than simply what we can see and touch; twentieth-century examples include infrared. We know it exists but we can't see it.

And the general consensus among physicists is that physics can only account for five per cent of the universe's matter; ninety-five per cent of particles making up the universe is known as dark matter or energy you can't see, nicknamed 'ghost particles' for their being hidden and undetectable by human devices. Its existence is inferred because, without it, the behaviour of stars, planets, and galaxies would be inexplicable. Meanwhile, scientists continually disprove things they have presented as fact, over and over again. So how can a scientist say existence is predicated on physical evidence?

Arrogantly, humans have long put themselves at the centre of the universe; the most intelligent beings that could possibly exist, with atheists rejecting the existence of anything you can't see or touch, like a parallel universe, a spirit realm, spiritual entities (entities which only exist spiritually, such as angels, who are at least ten-feet tall with huge wings, incidentally), and life in outer space. But to cut humans some slack, philosophical and spiritual notions require far deeper contemplation and a more objective and enquiring thought process than we generally exercise.

Atheists and sceptics often posit belief in God or heaven as a result of inherent human weakness; that we need belief in *something* because we can't bear the thought of there being nothing when we die. While belief may fill a gap for some people, that view isn't giving humans' intelligence and capacity for discernment, much credit.

In my mind, it made more sense that there was more out there than what we could experience with our five senses, and it was more extraordinary not to believe in a spirit world. I never understood why the existence of a spirit realm was such a hard concept for humans to grasp. So, when I started experiencing the spirit world for myself, when *believing* became *knowing*, it all made perfect sense. I didn't need to believe, I knew.

Then there's the question of consciousness – thoughts, feelings and emotions believed to be present in all sentient beings – and whether it is proof of selfhood or a soul? Are our thoughts produced by our brains? Or are our brains the vehicle for our thoughts to manifest in our physical bodies?

Many scientists and philosophers alike argue the former and struggle to explain how the brain produces thoughts and emotions which are unique from one person to the next.

For spiritualists, it's far easier to explain with the latter notion: consciousness is a sign of the presence of our spirit in the body and the brain is a vehicle for our consciousness. But it's still a complex, independent organ in its own right, so its physical activity can affect our thoughts. The reason there can still be brain activity when the soul has left the body is because it's still firing on a physical level. So, yes when a neuroscientist wires you up to a machine and detects brain activity even though your heart has stopped, this activity may reflect consciousness – the presence of your soul – but it could also merely be detecting physical activity. And, because our physical brain is a conduit for our consciousness, if the brain is damaged, such as through dementia or injury, consciousness may cease to be expressed, but this doesn't mean our soul isn't in the body still.

If science is correct and consciousness is produced by the brain (neurons, etc), then the assertion that Artificial Intelligence (AI) can mimic consciousness, or is conscious, or will be conscious one day, could be possible.

In 2024, it was widely reported that, following several big tech companies' research into whether AI is conscious or not, a report was published by a transatlantic group of academics predicting that consciousness will be evident in AI by 2035. In the final quarter of the year, it was also widely reported that there was consensus among thirty neuroscientists that there is a forty per cent chance that one day we'll be able to resurrect the memories from preserved (frozen) brain structures. Does this mean a revival in consciousness? A physical revival of the soul?

However, to anyone who doesn't subscribe to the view that consciousness is produced by the brain, all of this is a red herring, a misnomer, and the energy and resources being ploughed into all this research should be diverted elsewhere.

CHAPTER 6

FLORENCE

When I was eighteen years old I met Florence. We went to different schools but our paths crossed at a friend's Christmas house party and we hit it off after reaching for the punch. After a while, our time spent eyeing up the boys turned to a more sobering conversation about whether soulmates existed.

'I've just bought a book about soulmates,' I told her, 'and it says that more than one exists for everyone.'

'But that doesn't mean you'll find them,' replied Florence, always the voice of reason, I was to learn.

'Well, not if you keep talking like that!'

'What do you mean?'

In a far less articulate way, being only eighteen, this is what I told her... 'You know, the Law of Attraction. We are energy. The whole universe and everything in it, whether it's visible to the naked eye, or not, is made up of energy; all animate and inanimate objects *are* energy. And everything is interconnected because of this invisible force. So, our whole existence revolves around energetic vibrations.

'Just as scientists believe that the universe began with an intense build-up of energy, an explosion, a 'big bang', energy is all around us including mechanical, electrical, chemical, light, heat and sound.

'All living creatures have an electro-magnetic field within and surrounding them. Universal energy is the invisible life force which exists all around us. Just as energy swirls around us, energy flows throughout our bodies. We have seven major energy centres, known as Chakras (Sanskrit for wheel) which spin and keep the energy flowing, keeping us healthy in mind, body and spirit. Each of these Chakras has a distinct energy frequency and are linked to different organs.

'Our physical, psychological, emotional and spiritual well-being is all connected due to energy. And our energetic frequency, or vibration, is affected greatly by our thoughts and feelings, because thoughts, just like our actions, emit a vibrational frequency and, as like attracts like, if we are mindful about our thoughts and actions, then we can help create the life and future we want.

'We shouldn't underestimate the power of our thoughts and the impact they can have. In this way, through positive directive thinking, we have the ability to help others and bring about positive change. Thinking negatively about others, will only hurt us in the end.

'So, we need to be mindful about our words and our thoughts in addition to our actions, because they're very powerful.

'We need to align ourselves vibrationally to what we want to attract to manifest it; giving our attention to what we want, and not giving our attention to what we don't want, so our negativity doesn't become a self-fulfilling prophesy.

'If you're negative, that's the vibrational frequency you're emitting, so you'll attract things on the same level. But if you're positive, you're elevating your vibrational frequency. It's like, when you're walking around all grumpy, your grumpiness is just going to attract things to perpetuate your bad mood, until you snap yourself out of it, because, you won't attract happy people to you in that frame of mind. And when you're all stressed out, or flustered, you're way clumsier, like, you'll drop stuff or bang your head, which makes everything worse!'

When I finished this monologue, Florence replied, 'I just mean, there are seven billion people out there, but what are the chances of meeting your soulmate?'

I figured she'd had too much punch to be able to contemplate my speech on energy and the Law of Attraction, but seems I was wrong because she kept going.

'And what even constitutes a soulmate anyway?' she added.

'Someone you're not only attracted to but who's on your wavelength that you're spiritually aligned with, *meant* to be with, who comes into your life for a reason,' I said, adding: 'And of course, you can't find others until you've found yourself.'

It was this common interest in the deeper meaning of life and relationships that instantly bonded us. Soulmates are those we have pre-arranged to meet before life on the earth plane, who are destined to play a significant part in our personal growth and development. Florence was one of my soulmates. So was Sam. Our first meetings were unequivocally meant-to-be encounters and they were forever relationships.

While some encounters may be the result of circumstance or chance, and are of little consequence, there are other connections with people, be they platonic or romantic, which are meant to be. We have multiple soulmates throughout our lives. Our earthly connections with these individuals could also herald hurt, particularly if love is a necessary component of the connection, which may never be meant to last. Soulmates, like friends, can be ephemeral. At first I struggled with this concept, but when I got to my fourth decade, by which time I'd experienced plenty of cherished friendships come to an end, if a friendship didn't work out, I would shrug it off, knowing that that relationship had played its part and run its course. Relationships are fluid, they ebb and flow, come and go.

It was through Florence that I met Pearl, who was her mother Evelyn's friend. Florence lived in a rambling thatched cottage in the centuries-old fishing village of Beer. Her family's home consisted of two higgledy-piggledy adjoining cottages. The ceilings were low, the walls uneven and dark brown exposed wooden beams gave it character and charm. Pretty teapots jostled for attention in the kitchen window and passers-by would peer in to admire them. Black iron latches on each of the interior doors made a fuss when opened or closed, and there was a huge open fireplace in the main sitting room. But it lacked the warmth you'd assume a cottage with these quintessentially cosy character features would have.

Their cottage was where I had my first, unmistakable encounter with an earthbound spirit. You could say the way I learnt about the spirit world was a baptism of fire. It was often the case when I was developing my sixth sense that things would go unnoticed, or were dismissed as inconsequential or irrelevant. The lack of warmth in what should have been a cosy cottage was one small example. As time lapsed, I realised the relevance of it all and that the things we brush off as coincidences or imagination are often subtle signs and communication from spirit.

'I'm so glad you and Florence are friends,' Evelyn said to me, the first time I visited. 'She told me all about how you both couldn't stop talking all evening. Come on, let me give you a tour of the house.'

The cottage windows were small, preventing a lot of light getting into the rooms. Evelyn led me from their dimly lit kitchen, complete with AGA, deep basins and all the teapots, through the hall into a small, carpeted sitting room with modest open fireplace and then on into the adjoining, more spacious sitting room, with a huge inglenook fireplace and two sumptuous sofas. From here, a Crittall-style wooden door led out to a steep set of steps which rose up to a large tiered, lawned garden edged with flowering borders. The summer house at the top had a vantage point over the sea, which was a few minutes' stroll away.

A glass panelled door led into what would have been a separate cottage before it was made into one. The threshold between the two comprised two steps which led into a cool hallway with a dining room to the left and a staircase ahead. We climbed the stairs and ahead was the guest bedroom, while a corridor extended behind me to two bathrooms, and her dad's office, which you had to walk through to get to three other bedrooms. These could also be accessed from the staircase on the other side of the house. A map wouldn't have gone amiss in the early days.

To my left, a narrow wooden staircase led up to another spare bedroom in the eaves. While the stairs didn't feel any cooler than the rest of the house, when I opened the door, the room was as cold as a fridge.

'And this is another guest bedroom,' Evelyn smiled, striding in, pulling the corner of a densely floral bedspread even straighter. 'Florence's grandma likes to sleep here sometimes.' It was a pleasant looking, light, airy room. But I got bad vibes.

'Hmm, lots of light,' I grimaced, turning away so as not to offend her. 'Can I see the other side of the house?'

Having a strong sense, feeling or vibe – however you want to describe it – about something, is an indicator of your sixth sense firing. It's another source of knowledge which goes beyond the aesthetics of a space or a place, or the behaviour of a person. Physically, this room was pleasant by all accounts, but all I knew was that I didn't like this room, and I didn't want to hang around in it any longer. Ditto the staircase. I even narrowed it down to one step.

I mentioned it to Florence, who was as open-minded as me and was intuitive, and she admitted it had always been a cold room, but she hadn't got the bad vibes I was getting. But the bad feeling I got in the room was nothing compared with the feeling I began to get on the staircase leading up to it. One afternoon, I was sat in the living room on my own just chilling and tuning in, closing my eyes and opening my third eye, listening. My patience was rewarded, though not in the way I'd imagined. I was shown, in my mind's eye, a woman who'd had a stroke on the stairs, fallen, and died there.

It was a shocking sight and so vivid. That moment was pivotal for me in my psychic development. It was how I started differentiating between my imagination – which is you building or creating your own image – and psychic visions. When you're given something from spirit, you just know it's different.

I saw blood coming out of the corner of her mouth. I knew she needed people to know what happened to her, and the moment she knew I'd seen it, none of us ever had that uncomfortable feeling on the staircase again. It was as if she needed someone to know what had happened to her before she could move on to the Other Side.

As for the feeling in the bedroom, I got the sense that the former resident of the house, and former owner of the bedroom, a lady who had chosen to stay on beyond her passing, was quite uppity about someone else staying in her room. I sensed she knew she was well aware that she was dead and could go over to the Other Side if she chose. But she liked it there. Then one day, as if she'd simply had enough, she left.

A couple of weeks later when I visited again, the strangest thing happened when I left. I got into the passenger seat of my mum's car for the half-hour drive home to Exmouth, and someone else got in the car with us.

I could feel Simon's presence the minute we closed the car doors. It felt the same as when someone is standing too close behind you in real life. Instinctively, I turned around and looked over to the backseat of the car, but no one was there.

Evelyn and Florence took me to visit Pearl a few weeks later. Pearl and Evelyn had met through a spiritual healing circle in Seaton years before, the premise being that those with strong psychic abilities act as conduits to the spirit world and can channel healing energy – drawn from God, the Earth and ourselves – to those who need it. Evelyn would regularly drive the few miles up the road to pay Pearl a visit.

I was only allowed to sit in the circle when Simon eventually left.

But from that day forth, Pearl became my mentor throughout everything I would come to experience in the coming years, until she died.

CHAPTER 7

THE CELESTIAL BOOK

To say I feel lucky to have met Pearl, to have had her to consult with every step of the way and have as a friend, despite the fifty-year age gap, is an understatement. It was a privilege, and her legacy will live on in me, and all those she healed and gave advice to.

'Oh, rubbish, gal! I've only passed on what I've been told, that's all,' she would say, if she were alive today. Actually, she did say this to me when I talked to her in spirit not long after she passed over.

Despite spending countless hours over countless years giving spiritual healing – whereby the healing from the Other Side is channelled energetically through the hands of the healer to the recipient – both in person or absently, she expected nothing in return, while living on the breadline.

Often, when I'd sit with Pearl in her living room, it was as if the room became an auditorium. A crowd of people in spirit would gather all around the room above us, listening in on our conversations. We always wondered why they would find our conversations interesting.

Our being together would empower the other, and would allow us to connect with the Other Side more strongly and hear more clearly, than when we were on our own. Pearl explained that all mediums, while they're tuning in – and sometimes when they're not – are like beacons to the spirit world. Imagine a bright light, like a torch shining upwards into the sky, piercing through the clouds, through the atmosphere, transcending realms, allowing those in spirit to look in.

When we tuned in like that, I used to feel my head open up, like someone had been pushing on my forehead and then released the pressure. It was a weird feeling. In my mind's eye it looked like an iridescent blue-white prism rising out of my head, upwards into the sky, or the heavens.

But although mediums can converse with people in spirit, we are all connected with spirit. Thoughts about loved ones in spirit create beacons, channels, notifying those on the Other Side, who can stop what they're doing and listen to you. Telepathy is a real means of communicating with spirit and works between humans too, and humans to animals. The power of directive thought cannot be underestimated.

One morning, years after meeting Pearl, when I was driving to work, listening to Bob Marley in the car, I was completely immersed in the music, the sound of his voice, the words he was singing, connecting with the sentiment of his lyrics. And then, I felt his presence next to me. I could feel someone in the car, sitting on the passenger seat, filling the void in that cramped space. And for a few minutes, I felt pure happiness knowing that he knew his music still meant so much to someone whose life couldn't have been more different from the one he'd led in Jamaica.

This connection happened again with Nina Simone and Michael Jackson. Both these times, I was driving along, enjoying their music, and then, in my mind's eye, they would be there, on stage, lifelike, as if they were performing just for me, giving me a private concert, to show their gratitude for my appreciation of them.

The many horses Pearl had healed in her lifetime, and her many cats that had all passed on, used to visit a lot when we were sitting there talking. One time, when we were wondering whether there was other intelligent life out there and started talking about aliens and life on other planets, while we were talking, I was shown a huge lizard-like creature on a planet that was vastly bigger than ours. Pearl also saw the lizard in her mind's eye. He was working with a large machine, neither of us had any idea what it was for, and then, it stopped what it was doing and turned and looked round at her. Telepathically, without trying, we had connected with alien life, millions of miles away. She didn't feel they were more benevolent or evil than humans, just that they were infinitely more powerful.

My guide is called Quentin. Although I'd been hearing him, through my own intuition, for a long time before I met Pearl, it was Pearl who initially told me who he was and what he looked like. In time I could see him myself. He died when he was in his forties, not long ago in the grand scheme of things, in the 1950s. He is handsome, with light brown hair, and smartly dressed in tweed trousers and jacket and carried a leather bag. He is kind and wise; he'd been a teacher here on Earth. And he chose to be with me to help ground me and add a sense of calm to my wayward nature.

Often, people have just one spirit guide, while others have more than one. Some people like to call them guardian angels. On the whole, our guides aren't family or friends, but they are an excellent and deliberate pairing. And throughout our lives, our guides may change but, on the whole, they're here with us to stay.

'We don't make a habit of swapping around!' as Quentin told me, when I asked him if he thought he'd be with me for long.

Quentin told us that there are lots of universes out there, not just ours. And that while we live on the surface of our planet and can't see beyond our universe, there are other species living below the surfaces of their planets, who don't know there's anything beyond the surface of their planet. So for them to do so, would be like us getting to the edge of our atmosphere.

But, out there somewhere, exists a massive planet from which the inhabitants, the lizards, can see multiple universes. The lizards are friendly but they're at war with another alien race, giant ant-like creatures.

It was shortly after 11am one August morning in 2000, the cool dawn mist had long been burnt off by the mid-summer sun which was now high in a cloudless, blue sky, when we started wandering the lanes for one of the planet's most bizarre and mystifying phenomena.

Florence and I had gone to see Pearl and she told us about a vison she'd had of some crop circles nearby. They were made by the lizard-like creatures to send us a message that they were around, but meant us no harm. So, we went to find them. We didn't know what to expect. Our only experience of crop circles was from photos. I was intrigued to know how they would look up close. Would they be neatly cut? Would the stems be jagged? Would they be charred? Would their imprint be a huge let down, impossible to tell if they were authentic or a hoax; the result of village teenagers looking for a bit of fun? Would they be there at all?

We figured they had to be in a large enough field that they would evade the attention of the farmer or anyone wandering around its periphery. That was the only additional point we came up with ourselves to narrow down their whereabouts. But luckily, both Pearl and I got a strong sense that the field was close and we agreed upon the direction we should go.

'You know, if anyone knew we were out looking for alien crop circles they'd think we'd gone mad,' Florence laughed.

'Maybe it's madder not to believe that there is life out there,' I replied. 'Are humans really the most advanced, intelligent life force in the universe? What about all the other universes? The ones beyond ours?' I added, with a smirk.

Both of us were relying on being guided to the right place by Quentin. We wandered for about an hour and a half, the sunlight streaming through the trees and hedgerows, casting mottled shadows underneath our footsteps, passing gate after gate, sometimes on our left, other times on our right. We peered into any fields which contained wheat, and after hesitating for a few moments at each gate, I tuned in, and not feeling anything, we continued on our way.

Then we came across a gate which was so old it was only attached to its post by a single hinge and was tied up with tangled, fraying orange rope on its opposite side. As a result, it was leaning over, away from us, at an almost forty-five-degree angle to the field. The hedges on either side of the gate had become wild and unkempt, but the wheat was almost at its apex and ready to be harvested, probably in the coming days.

'It's this one,' I said to Florence, who was already fiddling with the rope.

'Typical,' she replied, observing the obstacle before us and flicking the rope away, 'let's climb over.'

The field was vast and sloped away out of sight, meaning there was a flattened-out area roughly around the centre, which wasn't visible from the periphery. We headed in, insects scattering, stalks splaying out, swishing with our strides, scratching our bare legs. After a few minutes, we saw something. Patterns cut into the sheaves. The patterns were neat, perfect almost, while the stalks themselves looked like they'd been torn, as opposed to trimmed with a sharp implement, or burnt. Slowly, we followed the markings, which in their entirety made up around a twenty-square-metre area. I pulled out my sketch pad and tried as best I could to record our discovery.

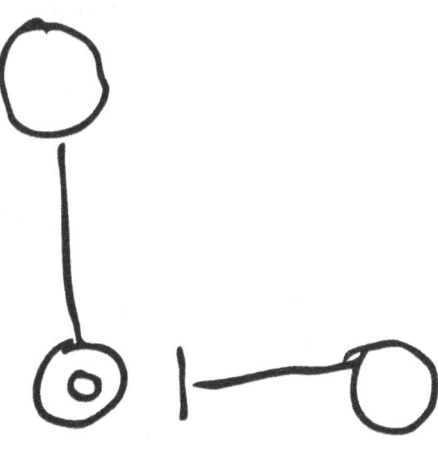

The number one rule of getting into heaven is that you never come back down to the planet and visit yourself. This would create a paradox that would result in the destruction of the entire universe, space and time. If you would disobey that rule, you don't get in.

There are a few reasons why there are earthbound spirits. Sometimes, a sudden passing, or someone taking their own life, can result in being earthbound. I was sitting in the pub near my house with a friend one evening when he started asking me about spiritual stuff. At this point in my life, I didn't have to consciously tune in; as soon as I started thinking about the Other Side I would open up, whether I wanted to or not. I felt a woman come close to me, standing right by my side in my mind's eye, but I could only make out her body, not her face. She was wearing what looked like a Victorian era dress.

The thing is, with your imagination, you know it's your imagination. When it's your mind's eye, it's right in your face. It's completely different; you know it's not of this earth. She told me that her daughter had died many years ago and, in her grief, she had killed herself through drinking. When I spoke to her and asked her what she wanted, she said, 'I'm waiting for my daughter.' She knew she was earthbound. I asked her why she didn't just go over to be with her.

I could see the path to the Other Side in my mind's eye and I told her, 'She's on the Other Side, I can see her, go there now.' But she kept saying, 'No, I need to wait for her.' I sensed that she felt that if she'd gone towards the light, she'd be admitting to herself that she had been waiting all this time, for so long, for nothing, and she couldn't bear this.

I carried on chatting to my friend, knowing she was still hovering around us. But later on, when I went to bed, I tuned in to talk to her again and tried once more to help her move on. 'Forget it all,' I told her. 'Your daughter is there waiting for you, right now.' And then, just like that, she said, 'OK,' and left for the Other Side. When I recall the story to friends, she comes to listen in. Our loved ones in spirit are always there waiting to greet us when we die and pass over.

Psychics are a beacon of light for earthbound spirits and they can see your energy and want to be noticed or heard. When you're really psychic, you need to ensure your guards have put up a protective shield around you and your home. I know my guards have put up a barrier around my home, and when I was thinking about the spiritual security around my house one time, I started to see how busy it was outside on the road, like a busy shopping street, spirits walking in different directions.

This is why inexperienced people shouldn't open a box of Oracle cards like Tarot and start reading without having an understanding, and appreciation, of spiritual principles. For example, it's essential to ask for protection first, and to close down properly, too. Because, the cards are like a portal to the spirit world, a beacon, drawing spirits close. Think of it as leaving your garden gate open to the street; nice people may come in, but also not so nice people. Self-protection and closing down is important when practising spiritual meditation, and Reiki too. A psychic state should be respected and entered into with care.

The first time Sam and I went to stay at my brother Robert's cottage in north Norfolk, situated on the edge of a village green, we were sat quietly in the lounge having a cup of tea, Sam was on his phone and I was flicking absentmindedly through a magazine, when I became aware, in my mind's eye, of people amassing outside the cottage. I tuned in to the vision I was getting of them gathering on the green several metres away and started to see them more clearly – women and children, men of varying ages, not of this era from the looks of their clothing.

I'd learnt to visualise a protective cloak around anywhere new I was staying, so I knew the cottage was well guarded and they wouldn't be able to come closer. But given how busy it had become, I visualised a stronger veil of light surrounding us and the cottage and then actively closed down my third eye, as if to tell them, no thank you, not today guys.

During a Remembrance Sunday service in the early 2020s, when the vicar was reading out some of the names of people in our town who had died in the Second World War, I had a massive tune-in. It was like the whole of everyone's remembrance and everyone's thoughts were being channelled through me to the Other Side to connect with them. I've never had a channel so clear before. It was like a huge shining glistening sliver light, a white-blue prism beaming up. I could see crowds upon crowds of soldiers who had lost their lives looking over us. The connection was so strong because of the collective energy. There was so much energy. It was hugely emotional. I was so immensely moved to be part of that connection.

There are also people who choose to stick around on the earth plane after they've died, like the old lady in the spare room. And others who choose to pop down and visit old haunts, so to speak. When they're visiting, it's possible to catch a glimpse of them.

When Sam and I returned to the UK from Canada, and before we moved to Devon, we settled in Bristol. It was while living here that I had one of my clearest ever visions of spirit. I'd gone for a run in the fields on the periphery of the south of the city where we lived. It was my usual weekend trail running route, and I was running across the final field towards home when up ahead I saw a man walking a large black and white Border Collie. They were walking along the path which I would soon join; on one side of them was the expanse of the ploughed field which stretched out between them and me, and on their other side, an impenetrable hedge. The other side of that was the housing estate where we lived.

I looked down briefly and muttered how it was typical a big dog was up ahead – I'd had an irrational fear of big dogs since being chased by a German Shepherd as a child – but when I looked up a moment later, they'd vanished. A minute or two passed and I was at the point on the path where they had been, so I slowed down to figure out where they'd gone and stared into the hedge wondering if it was an impenetrable as I'd thought. No gaps, no way through. I knew they were spirits.

This vision was when I was still developing psychically. The wonderful thing about having Pearl on the end of a phone was that every time I encountered spirit, I could check with her (and Brother Joseph) that it wasn't my imagination. It rarely was. On this occasion the man and his dog used to live close by and walked here when they were on the earth plane; they'd just come back for a visit for old time's sake.

Some earthbound spirits are people who had a particular grievance when they were alive, who had been so disgruntled with life that they unwittingly incapacitated themselves from being released from their anguish and torment. Almost like a self-fulfilling prophecy. People who have become so bitter that their bitterness has manifested in an invisible but nonetheless very real barrier, preventing their entry from this life into the next.

Time on Earth may appear linear, but our overall timeline isn't; it's like a ball of string, twisting and turning, hence the *déjà vu* phenomenon. Once you've moved over to the Other Side, you can come down and visit the earth plane, just not in the time you existed in your body. In this way, you live all your lives one after the other. You don't have just one life, then go back to the Other Side. You live all your lives along the timeline, then you go up, even though on Earth, decades or centuries pass between each lifetime.

Time has no meaning on the Other Side. We're used to things happening sequentially, but if time doesn't exist, how can things be sequential? On the Other Side, you don't feel the passage of time, yet things still happen sequentially. There are some things that are existentially ineffable for humans to comprehend, like the perception of other dimensions, and the miraculous conception!

We're all like seeds, popping up, and blossoming as we learn and grow.

Like suffering, life is a journey, providing endless opportunities to learn, grow, develop and progress. Who we are today is a result of all our past lives. The lessons we need to learn in order for soul growth are reflected in the hardships we face. It's up to us if we accept the challenge. We're all different. We all learn in different ways, and at different rates. You have to be pushed out of the nest to find your wings. Leave your comfort zone to find your capabilities. This development and learning persists throughout our lives on Earth when our souls occupy physical bodies, and continues when we're liberated from our shells of skin and bone on the Other Side. This is why we should avoid comparing ourselves and our lives with others; that person with the 'perfect' life may have had it rough last time.

We live in a reality where good coexists alongside bad. For example, we have amazing physical bodies that allow us to do amazing things, but, like with anything in physical form, there are limitations and imperfections, manifesting in degeneration and disease.

Ultimately, however cruel life can be, our biggest learning comes from the hard times, not from the good. The challenging times in life present opportunities – to develop personally or professionally, spiritually or emotionally. Through these experiences traits of our personality are unearthed, and we overcome things we never knew ourselves capable of. We find our strength, sometimes a strength we never knew existed. Often, from situations we feel are negative, for example an unpleasant work environment, a divorce or a forced house move, come positive situations. This is reflected by the symbolism of the lotus flower; from roots entangled in the murky depths below the surface of the water bloom beautiful flowers in the light above. This book wouldn't exist if this weren't true.

Our challenges and hard times are also opportunities to learn about others; often those are the times when you learn who your true friends are, because your hardships have given them an opportunity too – either to help you or walk away. So, our highs and lows and our suffering, give others around us an opportunity for growth. When you can see someone in need, do you wait for them to ask for your help? And when someone asks for help, is your default 'no' or 'yes'? Similarly, while you may find yourself wondering about the significance of someone in your life, you may have been the one playing a pivotal part in their life.

There may even come a point when you feel grateful for the suffering you've endured. That said, suffering and injustice are parts of life that pose an existential quandary, and reconciling with them is often beyond humans' psychic or emotional intelligence.

The divine, the spiritual realm, breaks all of humanity's physical and rational laws as we know them. So, some things will always remain a mystery, but that's OK. In a universe as vast as ours, it's to be expected. Just because we don't understand something, it doesn't mean it doesn't exist. If everything was fathomable, there wouldn't be a distinction between us and the divine.

On the Other Side, there are seven levels. How you choose to live your life on Earth, how you treat others and how much you learn, determines what level you are on when you pass over. Those that are on levels one, two or three will need to come back down to Earth again and learn some more. Those who are on levels four and up, have learnt enough in their earthly lives so they don't have to return, unless they choose to.

But that's not to say the learning ceases; on the Other Side there are infinite lessons to be learnt and these lessons continue once you're over there. Brother Joseph told Pearl I'd been down here a few times, but after the first time I chose to come back because I wanted to learn. Some people are brand new souls, like my brother Robert, who said he often felt like a rabbit in the headlights and really struggled with injustice and people behaving badly, like it was an afront to his new, unsullied soul.

Once on the Other Side, you have a 'review' of your life and get to see and feel the impact of your actions on others. Learning this gave me some contentment; that the bullies of this world will be forced to confront the pain they inflicted upon others. Work also continues over there too. Sometimes we are better placed to help others, to help the physical world, our planet, and the people we love, over there. So, once we've learnt what we came to Earth to learn, it's time to go.

On the Other Side, you still get to be with your loved ones on Earth, guiding them, supporting them and loving them. It's far worse for those who are left behind on Earth who are left with the grief of losing a loved one in their physical form.

Taking your own life doesn't mean your difficulties and trauma will disappear. The lessons unique to you, will remain, and you will likely have to return to Earth to work through them.

On the Other Side, we get to enjoy the things we enjoyed while on the earth plane, like walking in gardens or along beaches, and there are plenty of opportunities to socialise over there – I once had a vision of all my family in heaven having a sunny barbecue together! I am planning on spending a lot of time with horses over there, something I haven't had the chance to do on Earth.

One way work carries on when we get over there is becoming guides for others on Earth, if we choose to. There are a lot of people who care about you in spirit, not just your family and friends; all manner of people in spirit help us out at different points in our lives and most of them are unknown to us, but for whatever reason, they take an interest in us.

And Hell? Hell can be understood as a state of being, reflecting the actions of the deceased. Repentance is the way out. Hitler still walks in slime, apparently.

The question of free will, whether we are entirely free or not, poses an existential dilemma because it's intrinsically linked with the purpose of life; if we're not free to make our own choices, this makes us puppets, nothing more than pawns in a game of chess with God the Grand Chess Master, an age old analogy.

What determines how we make decisions is profoundly important because we can't be held accountable for our actions if we're not entirely free. One determining factor is our personality; who we are. But who we are depends on a set of circumstances – think nature versus nurture. Firstly, if our souls were all created, what decisions went into creating them? And who made them? Were we assigned any particular characteristics or inherent traits that would determine how we think, feel and behave? Then there are genes, that which we inherit from our parents which play a part in our physical, possibly psychological and emotional make up. Also, there are the broad-spectrum of experiences we encounter along the way.

If we can't control any of these things, how can we be responsible for our actions?

And are there various routes along one timeline?

The answer to this philosophical conundrum is that we get some control over our own creation. We get to choose our main personality traits. I chose to be sensitive, so this explains my empathy. Also, my temper! And we get to choose our parents. And our ending. Some people, for example, choose to be healthy their entire lives and have illness at the end (which could last several years), like all four of my grandparents.

There is an intrinsic link between mind and body; things are more likely to manifest the more attention you give to them, the more you let them be part of, or invite them into, your life.

Then there's how our spirit guides interact with us, how much they know, and how far they can influence us in relation to our freedom. They only get to see twenty-four hours ahead, so can warn us of impending danger, if we choose to listen, but only influence us through guidance.

One time when I was sitting with Pearl in her living room, I saw a beautiful 16th century house, that reminded me of Killerton House on the outskirts of Exeter in Devon. There was a library in it with floor to ceiling bookshelves. In the middle was a huge table, and on that table was a large book, reaching almost to the edges of the table. A group of men and women were standing over it. It contained details predicting how things were going to unfold.

But things can change. Predictions made by psychics are based on current circumstances. But people change their minds and unexpected occurrences happen all the time. And, then there's the butterfly effect. We cannot ever know the complexities of cause and effect between eight billion humans. One person decides something, which has an effect on someone else, and so on and so on. This is why those on the Other Side are so bad at predicting the future and aren't good with timings.

Perhaps an even bigger religious-philosophical question is whether God can act in the world. Because, if He can't, then how can He be all-powerful?

Assuming he is omnipotent, then He must choose not to? God stepping in is completely at odds with free will. Should He intervene in someone's life, but not another's? And if He were to act, imagine the knock-on effect. What He does could have ramifications that last decades or centuries down the line. Look at what happened when he sent his Son to Earth!

CHAPTER 8

HUMANS v MOTHER NATURE

By the time we left for Canada, the world had been up against it for a long time, attacked on so many fronts. She remained stoic, but was weeping.

Our lives play out in our own microcosms, our own tiny nooks in a gigantic world. For most of us, our choices revolve around sustaining our own lives and those of our dependents. Short term, at grassroots level, our lives are mostly impacted by our choices and actions, and those of the people we interact with; the cause and effect of things happening in our immediate environments. But we're also at the mercy of the choices and actions of people all around the globe, not only those in our immediate environs but those whose paths will never cross ours. In the 2020s, problems we thought were far away, like climate change and the whims of dictators, arrived squarely on our doorsteps.

The impact of geopolitical affairs and climate change well and truly caught up with us. For too long we'd dismissed the role each and every one of us play, individually and collectively, in the health of the planet – which we are custodians of – at large and civilisation as a whole. Whether consciously or unconsciously, we'd disconnected ourselves from the bigger picture.

The 2020s were a wake-up call to anyone who naively believed that what happens miles away doesn't impact them in their microcosm, their tiny corner of the globe, or worse still, didn't care about things that happen outside of their microcosms. For example, there was an escalation of unprecedented extreme weather fronts including wildfires and flooding killing thousands of people the world over.

In 2022 the Copernicus Climate Change Service reported that Europe saw its hottest summer ever recorded; multiple media outlets also reported that the Middle East, central Asia and China, South Korea, New Zealand, north west Africa and the Horn of Africa also experienced their warmest ever years. For the first time ever, in late July of that year, England saw record breaking temperatures of forty degrees Celsius, melting tarmac, grounding flights and warping trainlines, with fires destroying people's homes.

While parts of western Europe experienced never seen before droughts with the worst wildfires Portugal, Spain and Italy had ever seen, Somalia and Ethiopia in East Africa reportedly also suffered their worst droughts in forty years, believed to be exacerbated by climate change. Pakistan and India's record-breaking spring heatwaves were also believed to have been all the worse for climate change. Pakistan went on to experience record-breaking monsoon rainfall and flooding, reportedly displacing an estimated thirty-two million people. By September, a third of the country was underwater, with water-borne diseases plaguing the country.

Japan and Australia also saw deadly flooding, the USA saw heatwaves and hurricanes, and there were typhoons and cyclones elsewhere from the Philippines to India.

Then, just before Christmas a 'bomb cyclone' hit the north east of the United States. Temperatures plunged as low as minus forty-five Celcius in some parts of New York State, the worst hit area. Among the dozens of people whose lives were claimed by the storm were people stranded in their cars, as well as their rescuers. At its worst, it was reported locally that 1.8 million homes were without power in the US with some 200 million Americans under weather alerts, with the National Weather Service dubbing it a 'once in a generation' event.

As the year closed, scientists left us with the stark warning that climate breakdown was making our weather more extreme, and things were set to get worse they predicted – these weather events would be more frequent and more widespread. Meanwhile, world leaders grappled with whether any of the damage we'd inflicted on our world could be reversed.

Then, 2023 was hailed by the Copernicus Service as the hottest year on record and confirmed that for the first time, global warming exceeded 1.5C across the entire year. Ditto for 2024 and 2025, marking a decade of the hottest years on record with some of the worst wildfires ever experienced on parts of the west coast of the north American continent including California and multiple provinces in Canada.

At the world's biggest climate meeting, the 28th conference of the parties (COP28) in Dubai, United Arab Emirates, leaders pledged to fund those nations worst affected by climate change and, through transitioning away from fossil fuels, achieve net zero by 2050.

But then a spanner was thrown into the works when President Trump re-entered the Whitehouse in January 2025 and withdrew from the Paris Agreement – a treaty signed by almost 200 nations pledging to strive to mitigate climate change – and ramped up the extraction of fossil fuels, declaring, 'drill baby drill'.

We also had the coronavirus pandemic to contend with. COVID-19 emerged late 2019 in a town in Wuhan, China, wiping out almost seven million people across the world by the end of 2022. Whether deliberately caused or not – the jury's still out – it destabilised the world beyond its impact on our health, wreaking havoc politically, economically, educationally and emotionally. And it became a spectre in each and every one of our homes. Was this sickness a manifestation of the sickness within humanity, of our greed and selfishness, I wondered? The virus caused death and devastation. It also caused us to re-evaluate our lives, re-think the way we spend our time, and ponder the fragility of life.

The world was still reeling from the virus when Russia invaded its neighbouring sovereign country of Ukraine, about a fiftieth its size, on February 24th 2022. Once part of the USSR, Ukraine was one of fifteen socialist republics proclaiming independence from the Soviet Union in 1991. Not content with annexing and taking back Crimea, an autonomous republic on the southern part of Ukraine, in 2014, by force, President Putin instigated the war against Ukraine to take it back into his control. His subsequent bombs displaced, maimed and killed thousands of innocent people, including countless children.

So, what did this war have to do with countries thousands of miles away? The invasion of Ukraine pushed up the price of oil and gas, which pushed up food, fuel and energy prices. Exports of grain from Ukraine, one of the world's biggest exporters of grain to Africa's impoverished nations, dramatically declined, hastening famine there. Not to mention the threat of Putin starting a nuclear war; 'We're going to do something awful eventually' The Times newspaper reported him saying in September 2024. Then, other autocracies got involved creating more global instability. In November, North Korea reportedly sent around 12,000 troops to fight for Russia. This followed an intriguing swap of resources between two kindred spirits; Putin's horses for North Korea's Supreme Leader Kim Jong Un's artillery shells. Meanwhile, while not endorsing Russia's invasion of Ukraine, China's economic and technological support was instrumental in sustaining Putin's war effort.

Towards the end of 2022, the world's media reported that the then US president Joe Biden asserted that the world was the closest it had ever been to nuclear war since the Cuban Missile Crisis in 1962.

In the 2020s, it was widely believed that nine countries possessed nuclear weapons: the United States, Russia, France, China, the United Kingdom, Pakistan, India, Israel, and North Korea, with Iran busying itself to become the tenth nation with such lethal power. It was also widely believed that at this point that there were in excess of 13,000 nuclear warheads globally, ninety-two per cent in Russia and the US. Nuclear power exists to deter international aggression, yet there are far more weapons in existence than are needed for this purpose. It is estimated that an attack involving thousands of warheads at targets in the US would kill around two-thirds of the total population. Resulting mass fires would kill many more.

In a worst-case scenario, scientists predict that within two years of nuclear weapons being used, around three quarters of the remaining world's population would be starving due to the damage caused, because the smoke generated in nuclear conflagrations could threaten global humanity with nuclear winter. In this dark eventuality, gargantuan emissions of black smoke would block sunlight from reaching the Earth's surface, leading to frosts and subfreezing temperatures across continental landmasses for years, crippling any residual agricultural activity, and ending in mass starvation across the world.

Global unrest began a long time before Trump's return to power. Iran, widely regarded as a security risk to the whole world and deemed a 'criminal and terrorist regime' by the US, was reportedly supplying missiles and drones to Russia for its attack on Ukraine, and exporting weapons to militants, insurgents and pariah regimes throughout Africa and Asia,

And ever the pariah state, North Korea had begun intensifying its ballistic, cruise and hypersonic missile tests, reportedly firing more in 2022 than in any other year. In January 2023 Kim Jong Un apparently conducted a test of its intercontinental ballistic missile, the third known test of this long-range weapon in under a year. Reportedly flying 614 miles for almost 67 minutes, Jong Un said the test was proof of his country's ability to launch a 'fatal nuclear counterattack on hostile forces' and 'clear proof of the sure reliability of our powerful physical nuclear deterrent'.

And then there was China. Communist China has a long history of human rights' violations, for example, its oppression of the Uigurs and the brutal treatment of its political prisoners, while oppressing any beliefs it regards as a threat to its power: it is widely understood that the Chinese Communist Party regards religious faith as a threat to its rule and a challenge to its socialist values and wants religion to be wiped out in the country. For example, possessing a portrait of the Dalai Lama – Tibet's spiritual leader, who lives in exile in India – is illegal.

In 2023, the then US Secretary of State Antony Blinken postponed his planned trip to China – which would have been the first by a senior official in six years – following a Chinese surveillance (spy) balloon being sighted over the city of Billings, north west Montana. Tracking revealed it had flown over military areas. China, however, claimed it was a weather balloon which had blown off course.

On Saturday 4th February, 2023, former US Secretary of State, Mike Pompeo told BBC Radio 4's Today programme, 'The Chinese communist party has been at war with the West for at least 40 years, mostly economic…we just haven't recognised that China has declared war on reason, enlightenment and human dignity.'

He also told international media that 'President Xi of China wants dominance and is a bigger threat than Vladimir Putin'. He told Sky News: 'He wants hegemonic intent across the world with his Marxist-Leninist vision, and Chinese economic and political dominance in every corner of the world. That is his vicious objective. We have an obligation to the next generation to push back against it.'

On 15th November 2023, US President Biden met Chinese President Xi for four hours for 'blunt' talks about contentious issues such as detained US citizens, human rights in Xinjiang, Tibet and Hong Kong and Beijing's aggressive activities in the South China Sea. They agreed to 'high-level' communications, i.e. Biden said he'd pick up the phone whenever Xi called.

'Planet Earth is big enough for the two countries to succeed,' Xi told Biden. Biden was reported to have called Xi a 'dictator' within hours afterwards.

Then, while the War in Ukraine entered its third year, war erupted in the Middle East. On October 7th 2023, the terrorist Islamist group Hamas launched an attack on Israel from the Gaza Strip during which its members tortured and murdered around 1,200 Israelis and took about 250 more innocent people hostage. Declaring its right to defend itself, and its desire to wipe out Hamas in the Gaza Strip to protect its citizens, the Israeli military launched an attack on Hamas in response, and it was reported that in the first four months 30,000 civilians, many of them children, were killed.

In 2025, it was widely reported that many Western nations regarded Israel's prolonged response as disproportionate given the number of civilian casualties, and believed a two-state solution for Palestine and Israel was the answer to the bloodshed.

And then in June, Israel bombed Iran, fearing that if its nemesis succeeded in making a nuclear weapon – which it believed Iran was on the cusp of – it would obliterate Israel. Iran returned the bombs. Then the US got involved, bombing Iran's nuclear facilities. The world watched with bated breath to see how this terrible situation would unfold. And if a peace treaty was agreed between warring parties, how long it would last. Given the deep-rooted ideological gulf between Iran and its proxies and Israel and its allies, the situation was volcanic.

All the while, while bombs were dropping and bullets were firing, a silent war ensued. Cyberwarfare, involving attacks on computer infrastructure to compromise or destroy it, increased significantly from the mid 2010s with cyberattack tactics becoming more sophisticated, increasing the risks.

In the 2020s China was often cited as one of the main countries behind the most cyberattacks. China is believed to have long instigated cyberattacks against Western democracies, but in February 2024, the world's media reported that FBI Director Christopher Wray told the annual Munich Security Conference that Chinese cyberattacks on US infrastructure was at a greater than ever scale. He added that China's plan to secretly plant technology inside US critical infrastructure with the intent of disrupting or destroying it, had become a significant threat to national security.

And then in the spring of 2024 it was reported that the US Commerce Department had launched an investigation into whether Chinese imported smart/electric vehicles could pose a security risk; the concern focused on whether the cars' technology such as in-built cameras and other sensors could capture sensitive data allowing China to effectively spy on the West.

Also in the spring, the BBC reported that the UK government had accused China of 'malicious' cyber campaigns on MPs as well as the most significant cyberattacks in British history against the Electoral Commission in 2021. The then Prime Minister Rishi Sunak declared China 'the greatest state-based challenge to our national security'. China dismissed accusations against them as untrue. Nevertheless GCHQ, the UK's intelligence, security and cyber agency, revealed that more of its resources were devoted to China than any other single nation.

In 2024, Russia, Iran, China and North Korea were dubbed the 'axis of autocracies' and the 'quartet of chaos' by many Western foreign policy and military officials. And in June 2025, the UK government published its defence review concluding that the UK faced a 'new era of threat', warning of the 'immediate and pressing' danger posed by Russia and other countries including China.

The world was harbouring a fair few power-hungry warmongers, all ruled by their egos. It was an incredibly volatile time, and remained so.

CHAPTER 9
THE CARAVAN

Robert and I were brought up in a small three-bedroom semi-detached house on a housing estate on the northern fringe of the seaside town of Exmouth in Devon. My friend once said the estate was like the 'favelas of Exmouth' because, from the top of a nearby hill, the estate looked like matchboxes stacked on top of one another. Of course, he was joking. Ours was a family orientated housing estate where people went out to work every day. Deprivation was a short walk away, but so were the well-off.

After our parents' divorce, when I was two and Robert was four, we were brought up by our mum, who embodied the notion, 'Don't judge a book by its cover'. While diminutive in stature and self-deprecating in demeanour, she was immensely resilient and independent. A professional musician before we came along, she spent the rest of her life as a peripatetic music teacher. Her parents had both been teachers, so she valued education and learning, passing on the notion to us that education provides a ticket to autonomy and a better future, no matter your upbringing or social standing. There wasn't enough work for a full-time week, neither could she have worked full-time juggling single motherhood, so our childhood was defined by going without. It wasn't until my twenties that I realised it was a blessing not to have had it easy growing up; we were more aware of others' hardships, were more compassionate and more grateful, as a result.

Meeting as students at the Royal College of Music in the early 1970s, after some years in Scotland playing for a national orchestra there, our father, gregarious and funny, lived in London, where he continued life as a professional musician with a national orchestra, driving the 285-mile round trip to visit us every other weekend, unless he was on tour. In the early days he spent Saturday nights sleeping in his car a mile or two away on Woodbury Common. Lunch would often be a picnic of boiled eggs, cold baked beans and tomatoes we'd eat like apples, or he'd make us sandwiches on his lap in the car, cutting up cheese and tomatoes and buttering slices of bread on the white plastic lid of his sandwich box.

I was seven when he bought his first 16-foot caravan and towed it around East Devon in the pouring rain looking for somewhere to keep it. After a few hours, he found a pub on the old A30 near Exeter, surrounded by an acre of unkempt grass, and the owner let him leave it there for a year.

After that, he found a permanent base on a farm near Clyst St Mary. It was kept by the barns on a small patch of hardstanding, and that's where it stayed until we left for university. There was no electric hook-up this whole time. The black and white TV ran off the caravan's battery. It was always fuzzy because the aerial was a coat hanger. It was back-to-basics living in those days; me and Robert would take it in turns to fill up the 20-litre water container from the tap on the other side of the yard, hauling it back to the caravan, water sploshing over our feet.

So, our childhood was defined by walking in the woods and exploring the lanes, ball games, table football, hide and seek around the farm at dusk, and riding our dad's old motorbikes around the fields as teenagers. While we may have been 'poor' materialistically, we were rich in the support and attention we received from our parents who encouraged us to strike the balance between working hard and rinsing the most out of life's opportunities, and to strive to reach our full potential.

Pearl always maintained that some of the poorest people in the world were the most spiritual. While we were by no means anywhere near among them, it was no coincidence that among my friends, it was those who struggled the most who had the strongest sixth senses.

I developed an irrational sense of guilt later in my adult life when I was finally able afford to buy myself clothes and other items because I felt so bad that I was able to treat myself when so many people couldn't. I was wrong to feel like this: there is plenty of abundance to go around in the world, and just because you have something, it doesn't mean you're taking it away from someone else. And I used to think that praying for yourself was selfish. But it isn't. Love and support from spirit is abundant, both here and in the spirit realm. Indeed, reaching out to spirit and asking for help makes it easier for them to help you. And besides, praying for yourself means you're not expectant, nor reliant, on anyone else to help you. It reflects a will to be self-sufficient and take control of your own life. Furthermore, when we're happy and healthy, we're in a far stronger state to support others.

In 2023, research carried out as part of the World Values Survey, one of the largest and most widely used academic social surveys in the world, was published. It found that forty-nine per cent of people in Britain believed in God, down from seventy-five per cent in 1981, with around forty-six per cent believing in life after death. The survey included twenty-four countries: people in China were the least likely to believe, with seventeen per cent of the population saying they believed in God.

The same year, global market research and public interest specialists, Ipsos, conducted a survey into global religious beliefs which revealed that on average, across twenty-six countries surveyed, forty per cent of people said they believed in God as described in the holy scriptures and twenty per cent believed in a higher spirit, but not as described in holy scriptures. Meanwhile, belief in heaven averaged at fifty-two per cent and belief in supernatural spirits (angels, demons, fairies, ghosts, etc.) averaged at forty-nine per cent. The survey didn't detail whether there was a crossover, so whether those who followed a religion also believed in the supernatural.

So, in other words, according to this survey, while belief in God as prescribed by religions had declined, around the same amount of people believed in God and heaven as they did supernatural spirits, and for every person who called themselves religious, there was someone who believed in 'ghosts'.

Millions of people over the centuries, all around the world, have reported paranormal experiences, and most of the time, the themes are repetitive, describing similar experiences which have been turned into stories and become part of popular culture via books, television series and films. Take with a pinch of salt the bits where kids are possessed and start crawling up the walls like demons; this is fictionalised terror by humans who want their film to be a hit.

And yet so many people pass off others' testimonies and even their own experiences as imagination or delusion, looking to science as the definitive means of explaining all human experiences. But while science hasn't yet proven the existence of a spirit realm, it can't falsify it either; if scientists could put spiritual experiences down to the human brain playing tricks on us, hallucinations, paranoia, overactive imaginations, etcetera, then why haven't they been dismissed once and for all? Confirmation bias has a role to play here, whereby the way we respond to new challenging concepts depends on our existing views and beliefs.

This could explain why atheists who have paranormal experiences remain atheists. Like my dad, whose recollection of his first paranormal experience when he was living in Scotland in his late twenties with my mum, was one of the first accounts of the paranormal I'd ever heard and is not dissimilar from so many other people's.

'I was lying in bed next to your mum in our house in Glasgow,' he told us, when we were kids. 'It was pitch black, your mum was fast asleep, and I woke up in the middle of the night and heard footsteps coming up the stairs. At first I thought it was our next-door neighbours, but their staircase was on the outside wall so it couldn't have been them. The footsteps kept coming up the stairs and I thought, oh my god they're going to be in here in a minute. I heard them come right into the room, along the side of the bed and stop at the bottom of the bed. My hair was standing on end. I just thought, I've got to put the light on. So I carefully reached across and put it on. But there was no one there.'

Of course, it's impossible to know how many people have had a paranormal experience. There is rarely any evidential proof or witnesses. But we all know someone who has experienced something they struggle to explain. That's a lot of people!

The relocation or loss of an item is hard to explain away. Sam's rosary beads disappeared once. They'd been broken for a while, but he carried on using them when he prayed. Then one day, they vanished from where he'd left them on the mantelpiece in our home in Bristol. We looked everywhere, but they never showed up. Quentin told me Jesus had taken them over to the Other Side! He knew they were special to Sam, but it was time to get some more. As to why Jesus thought this clandestine theft necessary remained a mystery.

You'd think maybe our collective experiences, reflected prolifically in popular culture, may have been enough to make humans less sceptical. But it seems we are inherently fixated on evidential proof, and we struggle with the concept of the spiritual. Even people who admit they have paranormal experiences and don't have an alternative explanation remain unconvinced.

Our dad went through the majority of his life with a smattering of other paranormal encounters which he retold to us with no alternative explanation, but still struggled with the concept of a spirit world. One summer, while staying in a cottage in Brixham, south Devon, several notable things happened to him, including the sensation of someone leaning on his back when he was kneeling in the middle of the lounge floor reading the newspaper one afternoon. In the same week, he found the door latch repeatedly locked, despite him consciously leaving it open. And the radio would come on during the night. And plugs belonging to electrical items were swapped around. Someone was trying to let them know who's house it really was.

The first time I experienced something for myself was when we visited the Cornish fishing village of Boscastle as kids. According to folklore, centuries ago, 'witches' used to live there. Our mum had taken us here for a day trip in the summer holidays and we spent a couple of hours wandering around the tiny harbour and watching the sea crash against the rocks.

I felt a presence, an energy, that was a new and entirely unfamiliar feeling. I didn't realise it then as a thirteen-year-old, but this clairsentience, which can be described as a strong sense of intuition, would be one of the surest ways of experiencing the spirit world.

But it wasn't until I'd met Florence, and Pearl, that mediumship, communicating with and experiencing the spirit world, the Other Side, became part of everyday life for me. And it was only upon meeting Pearl that I learnt about guides, and how it was our guides who communicated with us most. Intuition, a gut feeling, and drop-in thoughts – that was how our guides and spirit helpers communicated with those of us who hadn't yet developed.

CHAPTER 10

SIMON

I WAS TAKEN COMPLETELY UNAWARE by Simon, who jumped in when I was trying out some self-hypnosis at Florence's house to help me relax in the lead up to my first-year university exams. Pearl since told me that opening up like this had taken my guards by surprise, giving Simon his opportunity. She said that he had had a fairly limited life here on Earth; he was in service to the owners of the cottage and died young, aged nineteen, about a century ago. He followed me closely, like he was living through me. In the beginning he annoyed me, then I learnt to live with him. But it took a while because his mischief needed taming.

The first hint of something not being quite right was the intrusive thoughts that would take me completely by surprise. On the drive home when my mum picked me up from Florence's house in Beer, I felt a presence in the back seat. I also had the thought to reach over and grab the steering wheel from my mum and swerve us into the hedge. I did wonder why I'd suddenly thought something so horrible but dismissed it and moved on to thinking about something else.

I talked to Pearl about it and she confirmed what I'd felt, that it was Simon taunting me. Not maliciously, just attention-seeking.

I continued to feel his presence, not constantly, but intermittently, for months. Simon came with me to university in Bristol. In my first year I lived in student halls of residence and there was one occasion in the autumn term when a few of us were sat together in one of our rooms chatting, and I had the thought that I could punch everyone in the face if I wanted to. It was such an odd, nasty thought. I knew it was Simon up to his tricks again.

He must have been with me for the best part of a year. Then one day, he decided to go, and that was that.

From then on, things got busier. I was speaking to my guides more and hearing them more clearly. Because I was studying philosophy, I was given Marguerite, who was French and had been a philosopher during her spell on Earth. And while Marguerite was very straight talking and unemotional, preferring to keep our conversations work-related, Quentin was a little more insightful when it came to matters of the heart, so I would make it clear who I was speaking to when consulting them on something.

I would hear them via drop-in thoughts at first, and then as my own voice in my head. I came to recognise that this was them speaking to me. That sense of knowing, and trusting in that feeling is such an important part of development, and took a lot of practice. In fact, unless you're clairaudient and can actually hear spirits talking like they're standing next to you in real life, like Pearl could, it's pretty much the only way you know the difference between a thought being your imagination or generated by you, and coming from spirit.

There comes a point when you can tell the difference between your imagination and a message from spirit. The distinction is clear to you. You just know. When you hear with your mind's ear the sound is as loud and as real as it is in the room, but it's within your head as well, it's like it's outside and inside of you. And when you see something with your mind's eye, it's far more vivid than your imagination; it's in your head, but it's accompanied by a strong sense that it also exists in the room, in reality.

I developed quickly to the point of talking to my guides whenever I wanted. Intuition and gut instinct precede that, and is something we all have. All it takes is an open mind. However, for as long as Pearl was alive, for important things, or notable experiences, I would always check with her. And, I would still have readings with other mediums for an alternative insight.

Almost all of my early, most vivid, encounters with spirit involved earthbound spirits. In addition to those who have chosen to stay or are visiting and passing through, sadly, a lot of earthbound spirits are troubled or not that nice, so haven't made it over yet.

I used to walk home from lectures through a small urban graveyard which slotted in between two parallel roads of terraced, three-storey town houses. One dark winter evening during my second year of university, I met a lady in spirit whose face I will never forget, and, despite my experience with spirit at this point and my robustness against the earthbound contingent, it remains one of my most shocking and frankly, petrifying, encounters yet.

I was deep in thought, walking along the path, which was illuminated only by streetlights from the surrounding streets, when a lady in an old fashioned floor-length, flowing dress, suddenly appeared and ran towards me. She had a look of terror on her face. Her eyes were almost completely filled with blood. As she approached, I too was overcome with fear, but not of her. She showed me how she felt when she died. I felt her fear. She'd been strangled to death where I was standing.

It was absolutely horrible, and really sad. I never sensed her again when walking that way. All she needed was for someone to know what had happened to her. Just like the lady on the stairs at Florence's house.

Sam's first experience seeing spirit clear as day was on our wedding day on May 24th 2008. We'd just got into the back seat of the car after the church ceremony, Robert was driving, and my friend, our photographer, was in the passenger seat, when Sam spotted a lady standing with friends and family waving us off along the lane. 'Who was that,' he said, as if he'd seen a ghost (because he had). It was my paternal grandmother. I knew it was her as soon as he described her – a tiny lady with a headscarf on tied underneath her chin. Sam said she looked shocked too, because she wasn't expecting anyone to see her!

While earthbound spirits may stay in one place, others pass through, or purposefully visit. Glimpses of them, shadows out of the corner of your eye, or a passing flash, shouldn't be dismissed as imagination. These ambiguous sightings are an indication that the witness is more in tune with the spirit world than they might have thought, or perhaps not thought.

There have been many times that I've seen spirits clear as day, like the man and his dog in the field. But unlike people in their physical form, seeing them never lasts long. I was unloading the car one day, outside the flat I rented in Bristol during my third year of university. The boot was open with half my shopping still in there. I glanced up the road and noticed a man in his 20s, casually dressed, walking along the pavement in my direction.

I decided I ought to be quick because my shopping was on show, so I hurried across the road, dumped the bags at my front door and looked up again expecting him to have reached the car by that point. But in those few seconds he'd vanished. A wall extended along the whole stretch of road, so I was left wondering if he'd legged it up and over the wall. Of course this wasn't the case.

Almost daily, while I lived in Bristol during university, I would see cats, not my cats in spirit, but other people's; they visited me because they knew I loved cats! And I'd see people in the hallway of my flat. Often they were in the form of dark shapes, or I'd detect movement out of the corner of my eye.

Relatively soon after moving into my flat in the second year, I was cleaning my teeth one morning and looked up and saw a man with long wispy white-grey hair and a gaunt face standing behind me, staring at me, right into my eyes. This is the clearest I've ever seen an earthbound spirit with my real eyes. I felt that punch-in-the-stomach shock, drew my breath and then turned around to find that, unsurprisingly, there was no one there. He'd made me jump, but he didn't scare me. I will never forget the look of shock on his face either!

CHAPTER 11
JOURNEY WEST

Sonny had just had his thirteenth birthday when Quentin told me the time had come to leave the UK for Canada. About six months before, he'd instructed us to withdraw as much cash as we could in case the banking network went down; if cash would even be relevant if society was to subsequently implode.

Some years before Pearl died, she told us that there would come a point when the dark side of humankind, the insatiable quest for power and control of a few, would destroy the world. She said the signs would include increased tensions between the world's autocratic powers, manifesting in ramped up cyberwarfare. Our guides would give us the warning when it was time to make a move. They would tell us, ahead of time, about the few places on the planet where we could escape the total annihilation of life on Earth. It would not be in her lifetime, she said, but it would be in ours. If we listened, if we trusted our intuition, we would get there on time.

Pearl didn't elaborate on how or why things would end but she did reveal that it would be the antics of one country in particular which would be the reason for the upheaval. An authoritarian state, past, present and future, a belligerent threat to its own citizens and the whole world. Ever the tech giant, this regime had been building up its cyber and nuclear powers, ready to strike and catch the nations it had long despised for having a different world view, off guard.

There was nothing panicked about our departure; the planning involved in leaving our lives completely behind with the prospect of never returning, was less hectic than the times I'd packed for a weekend's camping trip with Sonny in the same county.

But there was one problem with our departure. Sonny had been diagnosed with Type 1 Diabetes when he was nine. He already had coeliac disease, so diabetes was his second autoimmune disease, whereby the pancreas doesn't produce insulin, a hormone needed to regulate blood sugar, rendering it all over the place. This means diabetics are totally reliant upon artificially manufactured insulin (created from bacteria or yeast) to survive. Without insulin to bring blood sugar levels down to a stable level, the blood sugar would rise to deadly levels. Conversely, blood sugar which is too low can also be deadly for a diabetic.

Sonny was a Star Child, also known as a Crystal Child. I had a strong sense of this being so when he was a baby, and this was confirmed by four other mediums in his early years. Each one just came out and said it, with no mention or prompting by me.

Star Children are light workers and have the specific purpose of 'shaking things up' and challenging the negative behaviours of humankind to bring about positive change. They are very intuitive, sensitive, and often creative. Sonny also had the physical traits, like being smaller than average, with very blonde hair in his early years, and piercing blue eyes. The flipside of being a Star Child is that sensitivities often show up in health challenges.

After his diabetes diagnosis, Quentin gave me the following message: 'The map of his DNA has gone through massive changes recently. Neither are a life-sentence and he will be able to put his symptoms into remission, which is what he's chosen to tackle in his late adolescence. He'll be grand, he knows what he's doing. He's so connected to the animal and plant kingdom, they hold the answers for him. He'll know when the time is right and you're a wonderful guide for him.'

The problem for now was convincing the doctor to give us at least six-months' worth of insulin, needles and glucose.

Sonny had long been aware of how our lives were wholly entwined with the spirit world. His first experience was when he was three years old and we were in Brittany, northern France, on a week's holiday with my mum. We were staying in section of a woman's house which had been converted into an apartment and were having breakfast in the kitchen when Sonny said, 'Who's that?' He told us he'd seen someone, a shadow, walking past the doorway in the hall.

I got up and went into the bedroom he and his grandma were sleeping in on the other side of the hallway, and got a distinctly bad feeling. The energy in the room felt dense and oppressed. I immediately felt very angry that whoever it was, was trying it on with my son, as in, had made itself known to him, not myself or my mum. So, telepathically, I told it in no uncertain terms to leave.

I introduced my mum to Pearl soon after I met her and they became firm friends. Since she'd passed on, my mum would often speak to Pearl. On this occasion, my mum tuned in and heard Pearl say, 'We'll see it off'. Thereafter, Sonny often mentioned seeing someone walk past, the shadows of earthbound spirits passing through.

He knew all about our dear friend Pearl, and about what she'd prophesised two decades before, so, responding as if the impending world's end was nothing out of the ordinary, he duly packed a bag. Our concerns about the GP handing over half-a-year's supply of life-saving insulin was unfounded. He believed us when I told him we were going on a sabbatical and taking time out of school and work to travel. We just had to hope there was another supply at our destination.

It was June, and the morning was sunny and the air fresh when we set off for Heathrow, bound for Nova Scotia, the only last-minute seats available into Canada at that time. We'd been booked on flights to Vancouver, seeing as our final destination was in the western half of the country. But two days before we were due to leave, all the airports on the west coast of Canada and the United States closed due to malfunctioning computer systems. We were watching out for something like this and I was swift to book our flights into Halifax instead.

I told Sam, my brother, my parents, and Florence. The plan was for them to follow when myself and Sonny had arrived safely in Peace River. They booked their flights for a few days later and I gave them the coordinates.

When you descend over Nova Scotia, the land looks like a giant (beautiful) swamp; you can barely make human habitation out until you're virtually over the airport, it's a glorious verdant patchwork of pristine foliage and water.

The air was cool when we disembarked. Canada is slightly behind the UK when it comes to the seasons, so summer starts a tad later but lasts well into October. And the seasons are starker with sub-zero winters but temperatures hovering around thirty degrees Celsius in the summer across the land. The bits in between, fall and spring, are less protracted than in Britain.

Upon landing, we took a taxi to a car dealer not far from Halifax Airport and I bought us an SUV. All I knew was that we had to make it to Peace River Wilderness Park, some 5,000km away, about 500km north of the city of Edmonton. Whereabouts in this wild expanse of nothingness, and exactly how much notice the Other Side had given us, I didn't know.

In Canada, once you've left a town or city behind, there are miles of unspoilt, impenetrable wilderness, bar the odd farm or homestead, until the next settlement. It's not like Britain where footpaths and bridleways crisscross the countryside, or where the next hamlet, village or petrol station, is never further than a few miles away. But with the right knowledge and tools, you feel like you could easily create a sustainable haven in the wilderness here.

We headed north towards Highway 104 which would take us towards New Brunswick. From there we'd travel into the giant provinces of Quebec, Ontario, Manitoba and Saskatchewan before making it to Peace River in Alberta, about fifty-five hours non-stop.

I had a detailed road map but had also memorised our route and had plotted five stopovers along the way. We pulled into the first superstore we found, a Sobeys and bought supplies, tuned into a station playing soft rock (much to Sonny's consternation whose favourite band was Metallica) on the radio and set off.

We'd been driving since we'd arrived in Nova Scotia in the early afternoon, and, hungry and tired, it was dusk when we stopped at a motel parking lot, breathed in a lungful of warm New Brunswick air, and headed into the buzz of the adjoining bar and restaurant.

One of my all-time favourites, Iggy Pop's 'Passenger', was playing. We took a seat by the window and started musing over the menu. Poutine, battered clams and chips, ribs, burgers... all the Canadian staples were there. I ordered a Keith's pale ale and a diet coke for Sonny, and we chatted while we ate. We thought we were being discreet, but a lady with shoulder length wavy fair hair, I guessed in her late fifties, sitting in the booth behind us, overheard us and introduced herself.

'Well, hello you two,' she asked, 'you English?'

'Yes, we arrived today,' I replied.

'So what brings you to New Brunswick?'

She introduced herself as Marnie. I was just about to tell her we were embarking on a road trip of a lifetime and were en route to Vancouver Island via the Trans-Canada Highway, when Sonny beat me to it.

'My mum's spirit guide said we had to leave now before the world is nuked,' he said. 'Everyone, that is, who doesn't listen to their gut and find their way to one of the only safe places on Earth, in Alberta.'

Open-mouthed, my eyes darted from Sonny to Marnie, and I grimaced, wondering what she could possibly say in response to this cherub looking English boy spouting such a strange thing.

'Ah, me too,' she replied.

And so began our friendship with a kindred spirit. We finished our meals and went off to our rooms. In the morning, Marnie threw her bag in the back of our truck and joined us on our journey west. She had plenty of time to tell us her story.

CHAPTER 12

MARNIE

WHEN WE WERE KIDS, MY mum and dad used to run a spiritualist church in Fredericton. So there was always that belief that there was something beyond what we can see. I'm the fourth generation of mediums and healers in our family, as far as we know. My mum and dad were healers; my dad used to be able to heal in his sleep. My dad's parents were working clairvoyants and Dad's great-grandparents were working mediums and healers. But I was also brought up as a Christian.

Spiritualism was our way of life. So, when we – me, my two sisters, and my brother – were kids, whenever we said we saw something or had a vivid dream, it was believed and it was encouraged. Our parents would ask us more detail about who we saw. They'd ask us to describe the picture a bit better, for example, what the person was wearing and the circumstances, so we were already learning about mediumship.

My sisters saw and sensed things, but I was the only one who took it further and went on to become a medium. My brother moved to the UK and used to be a coach driver in Europe. One of his most vivid experiences was when he was driving through France past the Second World War graves. He used to experience quite a bit going through there, feeling very sad energy and seeing wandering soldiers. That was quite moving for him, he never spoke much about it.

I was about three when we moved to Fredericton from Lakeville Corner out in the sticks and I saw more and more people out and about, who were there one minute and gone the next. I was about seven when I started seeing a soldier in a sentry box at the end of the bed, every single night. It terrified me. I never ever told anyone about the soldier stood at the bottom of my bed.

When I told my mum, only recently, she said, 'That explains a lot, because you didn't want to go to bed.' But he was there to protect me and was watching over me. He was so vivid it was like he was looking right at me. That used to scare me. It went on for about eighteen months until one day he wasn't there anymore. He disappeared, a few months after my sister was born; the energy changed.

When I was about six, the only negative experience I've ever had with spirit occurred. I went upstairs to get these silver bangles from my room and when I was at the top of the stairs, about to come down, I felt a hand push me in the centre of my back, and I fell downstairs. This has been the only negative thing to ever happen to me in my whole life because I came to sense spirit earlier on. I tell them off if I feel any threat.

As a child, my experiences with spirit were sporadic. My sisters and I used to play with toy zoo animals and every night we'd set them up on the dressing table in our bedroom. And in the morning, they'd all be knocked over, lying on their sides. There was a little boy in spirit in the house who came in to play with them when we were asleep.

At school I was always daydreaming and looking at the shapes in the clouds, I always had this feeling I should be somewhere else, like I didn't fit in, a square peg in a round hole. I didn't have many friends, so I was always wishing I was elsewhere. I spent a lot of time in this altered state to get through the day sometimes.

When I was about eight I was bullied at school because I was a bit different. One day I was playing on my own, some distance away from anyone else, inside the school at the bottom of a set of stairs, and heard a booming voice say, 'Life's a game' in my mind's ear. It was really loud. I said, 'You don't have to shout at me!'

It's stuck with me all my life. When I've felt fed up, remembering that is what's got me through difficult stages of my life.

In my forties I lived in the Caribbean for a while as my husband had been posted there. Things hadn't been right between us for a while, but I had no plans to jump ship. One morning I was drying my hair in the mirror and heard, 'You'll be home by Christmas'. We had no plans to leave and come home early. But we were home by Christmas. Not long after that we got divorced.

When I was a teenager, the small spiritualist church my mum and dad ran was from a little room above a garage, so us kids would go every Sunday to church meetings. My nan and grandad would come and stay and do the Sunday service, and the night before they'd have a healing circle at home. We weren't allowed to sit in it but we used to sneak downstairs and my grandad used to go into trance and we heard him get a lot of information about how plants and herbs can aid the healing process.

Every Sunday we'd trundle off to church and our parents would feed us sweets to keep us quiet. I was twelve when I had first message given to me: 'You can lead a horse to water, but you can't force it to drink.'

I was about fourteen when a couple of friends came over to play and said they wanted to do some Ouija stuff. We wrote names on bits of paper and I went out to the kitchen to get an empty glass, and my nan came in and told us off saying, 'You don't know what you're messing with.'

My dad got us gazing into the fire to try scrying; we saw faces popping out of the flames and patterns in the curtains. He was teaching us to open our third eye. The messages through these patterns could have been from our guides, loved ones, or people in spirit who just wanted to help us learn and develop.

Scrying is a way of opening up and accepting what you see. When you set out to be a medium you can be so desperate to see something, you don't get anything. You have to be relaxed to be able to see. You're like the telephone exchange. You're the one plugging in, passing on a message.

I'm clairsentient, so I feel or sometimes hear spirit. During a reading, my guides help keep those in spirit in order, so they're not all jumping in and giving mixed messages – I tell them to line up in order! And I'm claircognitive, when messages get dropped in to your mind.

I have two guides, a Native American called Red Cloud, and a small Mandarin man who has his hair pulled back in a long thin plait and puts his hands in his sleeves.

I started going to a developing group in my mid-thirties. I had kept my mediumship dormant for many years partly because I was going through a difficult time with my husband. One day my parents asked me if I felt like going to a meeting. That reintroduced me to the spirit world. The medium told me where my lost earring was, and when I got home it was exactly where he said it was.

I opened up more when I completed my massage and aromatherapy courses. And then, age forty-two, I started using mediumship in that work. It was second nature. I knew where my clients were holding energy in their body, where their aches and pains were and what emotions were associated with their physical pain.

Predominantly I'm a healer and Reiki Master. It's always been there. I was watching *'The Incredible Journey of Doctor Meg Laurel'*, a film about a healer with my dad when I was fifteen, and I said at the end, 'That's what I want to be.' I knew I had to be a healer and help people.

I started mediumship development groups at my home for people and took over hosting the town's spiritualist church from my parents. One of my mediums dropped out on the day and with no one else available I thought, 'Oh well, I'll have to do it then!' I told spirit off though, saying, 'How can you do this to me? I know everyone's stories, this isn't fair!' I was fighting it every step of the way.

Come the evening, I told my mum she'd have to chair the service in place of me so I could do the mediumship. And then six new people came in and I didn't know anything about them. So that was my initiation of becoming a platform medium.

I always know where I'm going. I scan the room and get fixed on someone and you know you're with them because everyone else disappears. It's as if no one else is in the room. I used to think, 'Where have they gone?' You're literally passing on the information you're given.

There have been times when people haven't wanted to accept the message I'm giving them. But I know I'm getting it. When they say they can't take it, it makes you doubt yourself.

On one occasion, I'd given half a dozen pieces of evidence out, and thought I was with this woman but she, and no one else, was taking it. The lady in spirit with me was being persistent, and then she said, 'Just tell her, Edna!' And then all of a sudden, the woman I thought I was with jumped out of her seat and screamed, 'That's my mum!' Then she said she could take the rest of it, after all!

I must have been a platform medium well over fifty times now, and done hundreds of readings over the last twenty years, via email, phone and face-to-face.

A medium is there to prove life after death, that we all go home to the maker and that life goes on – to give guidance in your present life to help steer you on the right path, and gently take you in the right direction. They can't interfere with our lives unless we ask for that help. They're not here to predict our future.

Mediums are psychic but not all psychics are mediums. Mediums are there to communicate with loved ones in spirit. They're like telephonists passing on a message. A psychic can pick up on feelings and energy but can't communicate with spirit.

A clairvoyant can see into the future, but nothing is set in stone. It depends on you and other people; others involved can upset the process. Mediums see a probable future based on the now. They're also tapping into your dreams and desires.

If you want something, you need to let go of that want. That's the hardest part of being human. Trust that when the time's right, it'll manifest in your life. By wanting, you're not being receptive.

You need to accept that it's already done. If you're wanting, it's still out there. Just for one day, believe it's already happened. Try this: say the word 'Accept.' Now say, 'I want.' What's the difference between those vibrations? Accept is gentler, more open, isn't it?

Everyone's at different levels in their belief system about how things work. The same thing happens in the spirit world; we're here to learn, to develop, to become more at one with Source and to open our hearts to love and share that love. If you have a closed mind, it can be blank, you might not see anyone, because you think there's nothing else until you start to wonder. Then the light comes in.

Energy and spirit are all around us. It's not in the next room, or over there, it's everywhere, it's part of the air we're breathing.

When I was working as a carer, I would sit with an old lady, lovely Annie, who was scared of dying and being on her own. A fellow carer and I were just cleaning her up and putting her back into bed after lunch when the light dimmed and I saw an orb, a spirit coming out of her mouth. I could feel that someone was waiting for her behind me. We left her alone and went home as our shift had finished and I just knew she'd passed away. Half an hour after I'd got home we had a phone call to say she'd passed. I felt privileged that she'd waited until I was there.

In one of the houses me, my husband and our daughters used to live in, there was a man in spirit who used to live in the house and didn't like us being there. It took him a couple of years to really make himself known; my relationship with my husband was coming to the end and so the heightened emotions were enough to bring in that energy. I knew I had to deal with it because he was making the house uncomfortable; the kids were hearing footsteps up the stairs at night and I would feel chills, like something passing me, in the house.

Then, one day, I heard a disembodied voice like it was in the room, say, 'This is my house, get out.' Everyone was out, so I thought, right, this is the time to deal with him, so I replied, 'I'm ever so sorry to tell you this, but you're dead and it's my house and we live here now, and if you're going to be mean to me, there isn't room for both of us.'

Next, the kids' toy cars came flying down the hallway at me and a marble flew past my ear. Then for about half an hour we spoke. As if he was in the room, again I heard, 'I'm not dead, I'm very much alive,' to which I replied, 'You're dead in this world, you've passed over, you don't own this house anymore.' I asked him, 'Is there someone around you, who you used to love?'

'No, I'm on my own,' he replied. I thought, this is like talking to a child, he's so defensive. I told him, 'Open your eyes, there must be someone around you who loves you?'

A few moments later he said, 'I can see my mum. She's been dead years.'

I asked him what she was doing. 'She's got her arms open,' he said. I could see him and his mum in my mind's eye. I had been hearing him in my mind's ear until he realised he could converse with me telepathically.

I'd been taught how to help spirit move over into the light. I get them to look around to see someone they know, someone who would have loved them. Love emits such a high vibration it becomes a light they're drawn to. We encourage them to go towards that light energy.

He described his mum with her arms open waiting to give him a hug. I said, 'It's OK, go and have a hug...' I talked him into it, and off he went. You could feel the energy in the house shift as he went. I just got on with my day then, thinking, that's that done!

After I got divorced, the kids all heard footsteps again. This time it was their grandad looking after them.

A lady asked me to come to her home to conduct a clearance after she'd been kicked in the leg by someone in spirit. When I was there, I too felt someone kicking my leg behind the knee. It was a child doing the kicking, a little boy who wanted to be acknowledged.

The lady later told me she'd had a miscarriage. The little boy was growing up in spirit. While the lady was still grieving the miscarriage of her child, the boy wanted to let her know he was fine and not to worry anymore or feel sad. He wanted her to shift her energy out of that negative 'woe is me' mindset, to 'It's OK, I'll meet you again.' Every time she was sad and depressed, he was with her. He was in and out of the spirit world to be with her.

If spirit want to get through to you, they will get through to you, even if it takes them years. You may feel something strange is happening but if you ignore it they will work in whatever way they can to get noticed. That's all they're there for, not to cause disruption, but to pass messages on, sometimes simply, 'I'm OK.'

You can raise more energy together if you want to give healing. Hold hands in a circle, visualise a channel of light in the centre of the circle and imagine anything you want being put into the light, so it can be healed. Then that light gets gathered up and taken back into source energy along with anything and anyone who needs to go with it.

When I've been asked to help move a spirit on somewhere, I get everyone there involved as a collective. Most people can feel a shift in energy happen, and feel peaceful afterwards.

There have been times when I've been healing and seen a dark mass coming out of people. On one occasion I went to help a woman and saw a darkness, like a black treacle, oozing up out of her solar plexus. I told myself not to be scared, just to go with it. I've seen this sort of thing since, but not to that extent. It was pretty gruesome.

I've seen lots of nature spirits. My friend and I would walk in woods and then sit and do a little meditation to open up our third eye. Then as we sat there we would see energies swirling in the water. We wouldn't tell each other if we saw something, we'd just say, 'Look over there,' and then we compare notes afterwards and find out we'd both seen the same thing.

On one occasion, my dog JD went off for ages, but I'd forgotten about him because we'd stepped over a natural boundary created by some branches into a space with the most beautiful magical healing energy. I suddenly thought about JD and knew the fairies had taken him off. When he came back I asked him telepathically if he'd been with the fairies and he had the biggest grin on his face.

Every plant and tree has a spirit component too, helping them grow and mature, bear fruit and bring forth for the next generation. Sometimes I've seen their spirit guides, it's a privilege to have been shown them. You have to be in a space of acceptance to see them. You can want to see them as much as you like but you won't unless you're in the right space.

One day, I saw a pointy-faced man at the bottom of my garden. And in the woods we've seen little earth-coloured dragons. To see such entities you need to be open to what you might see today. Follow your intuition and it will lead you where to go.

My friend and I had been sitting by the side of a river one afternoon and when I got up to go, I was pushed on my shoulder and fell down the slope. This made us laugh so much. We thought it was the water sprites because we'd watched them dancing on the water earlier, so we knew they were having fun. You know stories of Jack Frost? The depictions of him with a long gangly body? They look like this. They help keep the waters clear, and help Mother Earth. We do so much damage to her.

I've always believed in Jesus. When Dad gave up the spiritualist church, I joined the Salvation Army and started teaching at a Sunday school. Now it makes me laugh; the Bible is full up of made-up stories. Jesus's life has been distorted by men. Women were written out from the 3rd century, but there were a lot of women who worked alongside Jesus, and women were integral to passing on the message of spreading the love of Jesus.

The Bible is a teaching tool about how to love and how to live. All roads lead to Rome, none of the religions are wrong.

CHAPTER 13

SMALL SIGNS

W E ALL HAVE A SIXTH sense. But the majority of people don't pay any attention to it. A strong intuition, a sense of knowing, feeling things energetically, are traits of being psychic. There are psychics and mediums. While psychics use their intuition to receive information and can read energies, mediums can communicate and connect with those in spirit.

Intuition is the main way we can all be in tune with our higher selves (our true soul essence, our 'best self'), and with source energy, God. It's your inner voice. The means your higher self, which knows what is good for you, or your spirit guide, transmit the truth to you, through inner seeing, hearing and knowing. Through your intuition, you can discern the difference between your higher self and your ego, which is our less conscious self, constituting less mindful behaviour.

Listen to your intuition and you'll find out what you need; what activities and what people are good for the nourishment of your soul, and which direction to go in. In this sense it's bossy; listen, and you'll hear it tell you never to change or abandon yourself to please others, especially those who don't appreciate you. Instead, don't be hindered by others and go on your merry way. Life's struggles make it harder to hear our intuition. So does our ego. But the process of falling and rising up again, sharpens it. And the more you listen to it, the more you strengthen it.

One of the biggest achievements of developing spiritually is arriving at the point where you know the difference between your imagination and intuition. There came a time in my forties when I realised that over the last decade of me asking other intuitive friends for their opinions, or even visiting mediums for readings, that the only person who'd been right all along was me. But you can't force this. Knowing is a process. And when you know, you'll know you know! A beautiful description of intuition can be found in *Women Who Run with the Wolves: Myths and Stories of the Wild Woman Archetype*, by Clarissa Pinkola Estés.

My great maternal grandmother trusted her intuition when my grandpa returned from his posting in Egypt during the Second World War. During that awful time, no one knew if and when their loved ones would return from duty. But she did. The day Grandpa returned to his parents' house in Ilfracombe, north Devon, he walked through the door and was met not only by his mother, but by the scent of her cooking. She had baked him his favourite ginger cake for his homecoming.

Sometimes, we may create blocks or barriers to receiving information intuitively. Blocks can happen if we're very upset or through stress. Or if we feel very strongly about something. Sometimes we may be told something but not want to hear it. This happened to me a couple of years after I gave birth to my son. I was hell-bent on becoming a surrogate mother. I went through the entire, months' long process and was at the point of considering my couple. I was convinced it was the right thing to do because I hadn't wanted to hear anything to the contrary. It took another medium friend to step in and boldly inform me that my loved ones on the Other Side were adamant that I shouldn't go ahead with it, because I would 'never come back' from giving away a child I bore, even if it wasn't genetically related to me.

One thing which came as a surprise, perhaps naively, was that not all psychics are nice. I just figured that if you were intuitive, this meant you were empathic and therefore nice. But the two don't go hand in hand. The usual human traits prevail in us all, whether we're psychically developed or not. And there are those who even use their psychic gift to manipulate others; spiritual practices can attract those who have suffered trauma, are vulnerable in some way or are searching for meaning, and sadly there are psychics, real or false, willing to play on people's vulnerabilities for their own gains.

There is also a lot of pseudo-spiritualism going on in today's society. A well-meaning shift towards mindfulness, holistic and alternative therapies from the Noughties onwards gave rise to an increase in two groups of people, those who were well-meaning but ignorant, and those who were disingenuous but keen to be part of the zeitgeist and masquerade as being empathic and spiritual when actually, they lacked discernment for both. Actions have always spoken louder than words.

Developing your sixth sense, listening to your higher self, your soul essence, takes work and practice and as you hone your intuition, it should be accompanied by humility. I've met plenty of intuitive people that lack both of these qualities and therefore think that it's intuition when it's actually their ego talking. As Jesus said, 'Beware the false prophets.'

Manifesting – the notion that positive thinking will yield positive outcomes – became trendy post coronavirus pandemic; in 2020 Google searches for the buzzword multiplied by 669 per cent. But, really, it's one and the same with the older notion of the Law of Attraction; the energy you put out into the universe will attract that vibrational frequency back.

Does manifesting work? There isn't a simple answer to this. Ask someone who won the Lottery and they may say yes. Ask someone who has toiled long and hard, who may or may not have reaped what they've sown, and they'll probably say no. But it's not as simple as yes or no. There is too much at play, for example, the will or behaviours of others and your own actions, which may or may not be aligned with your thoughts.

Here's the thing: manifestation is about creation but requires the alignment of mind, body and soul, and the release of negative emotions stored in your fascia – a thin casing of connective tissue that surrounds all our organs, blood vessels, bones, nerve fibres and muscles, holding them in place – in order to receive. Your conscious mind may say one thing, but your subconscious is the most dominant and will always win. It's your baseline vibration, so if you're storing long-term negativities, they'll override any superficial attempts at positivity.

As for manifesting bags of money, money is an emotionally charged topic, but money moves to people who know how to move it. And, it's easier to manifest more money when you've got money! Money is like water, it doesn't want to be held, so we need to let is flow away from us, and to us, not let it stagnate.

Somatically – the relationship of the physical body and the mind – you manifest by being present in the moment and feeling that sense of ease and receptivity to be able to cast your energetic net out to catch what you desire. Contrary to popular misconception, expectation blocks manifestation because if you expect something you're chasing it, and if you're chasing it, you're chasing it away.

Some of manifestation teachings remove God, but we are not separate from God.

Does the Law of Attraction work? As this is more about energetic vibrations, and attracting things and people on your wavelength, then, yes. But there's also the Law of Reciprocity; in order to receive there has to be that flow of going back out, a balancing of energies.

Either way, daydreaming and fantasising, visualising things that make you happy, is certainly not a waste of time, even if it's not appropriate in the classroom or the office! And, thinking positively and having gratitude don't just raise your vibration, making it more likely that you'll attract positivity, but they pave the way for acceptance, contentment and therefore improve your wellbeing.

Self-development begins with noticing the more subtle signs. Our spirit guides are always trying to communicate with us. Things we pass off as chance and coincidence may well be them sending us little messages. Oracle cards are a means for spirit to communicate with us. The first time I ever used a pack of Angel cards, the same card, 'Patience' (something I've always lacked!) came out three times in a row, despite my rigorous shuffling. A little sign from spirit to show me that they were to be trusted. I've always marvelled at how accurate the Tarot is, every time I've read for someone.

Have you noticed how there are some things which fall into place relatively seamlessly, with little effort? This is the universe aligning. And then there are those things which don't work out, no matter how hard you try? Sometimes, something is not the right course of action for us, no matter how much we think it is.

But these experiences, the ones you work so hard at, and maybe perceive yourself failing at, are the testing experiences which help strengthen our resolve, are soul building, and are the ones we learn the most from.

Health scares, like the Pandemic, although horrible and scary at the time, prompt us to stop and think more deeply about our lives and how we're living them, to reflect and take stock. For many of us the Pandemic gave us a demo into slow, mindful living. When we overcome illness, or have to live with it, we're reminded to appreciate the small things, things we took for granted, drawing our focus into the present moment. For that is all we have.

Frustratingly, if you search for meaning in the midst of your journey, it is likely to be extremely difficult to discern why something you want so much isn't working out. 'It doesn't make sense, I don't understand!' is something I've said many times. But then, weeks, months or years later, it becomes apparent; you realise that something didn't work out back then because it was for your own good. That said, there are a few things that, a decade on, I still didn't find the answer to. But faith in a higher order includes trusting in timing as well as trusting that things are as they are supposed to be, and that things will work out for the best.

For example, Sam and I put offers in on four houses during our marriage; all of them fell through. But, what with the ever-rising property market, had we managed to buy one, then when we separated, we would have made around £100,000. Instead, we continued renting, draining our savings. We accepted, without ever knowing why, that these houses obviously weren't meant to be. And yet, the week we decided to live apart, Sam found a flat to buy on the same road as we were renting and moved in within two months. Everything flowed with ease. And his place was number 11A, the same number, and the exact same entrance and hallway set-up as my favourite pub, back in the day. Small signs!

In a period of about five years, I went for close to 150 jobs. I had about a dozen interviews, travelling hundreds of miles across the south the country to attend them. I was offered two, but had to turn them down due to the salaries being so low that I would have been in the negative each month! It was a gruelling few years. And I ignored my intuition for most of it: I never wanted a full-time job which would have meant putting little Sonny in childcare for 40 – 50 hours a week. I thought it was the moral thing to do, financially.

All the while, as a freelancer, I was dealing with undermining, oppressive egos in the work arena. So, eventually, I listened, took a leap of faith and set up my own business. From that moment on, everything flowed and went from strength to strength. I always heard that I'd get a 'very good job'. They just didn't specify that I'd be the one to give it to myself!

From roughly the point where our marriage became unsettled, I began to see the number 11.11 a lot. While my work as a news editor was extremely fulfilling, my personal life was less so. I started seeing it at least once a week. I didn't think much of it until months later when someone posted the meaning of 11.11 – that the Other Side is letting you know you're being looked after and are on the right track – on Facebook. Ever since, this auspicious number showed itself; through enduring struggles, including my separation from Sam, giving me confirmation that I was on the right path, despite it being a rocky one.

There are signs in nature too. Indeed, being in nature boosts our psychic intuition as we can draw upon its beautiful energy. When birds, particularly robins, flutter up close to you, they have usually been sent by a loved one in spirit, so too, little white feathers. A favourite or poignant song popping up on the radio, in a supermarket, or wherever, shouldn't be dismissed only as chance either. Connections and signs can come in all sorts of ways. When I booked a week away in an Airbnb in north Devon for a weekend by myself to write, it only occurred to me when I'd returned home that I'd been staying at the same address as my late maternal grandparents, albeit in a different town.

Our guides are always trying to help us. So next time you get stuck behind a tractor when you're in a rush, be grateful; this could be them trying to avert an accident.

Then there is also the not so small sign of physical touch, perhaps the hardest contact from spirit to write off as imagination. My most vivid experience was when Sam and I lived in the flat overlooking the sea. I was lying in bed asleep in the middle of the night and woke up feeling a hand gripping my wrist and then rubbing my arm.

Thinking it was Sam, I stretched my arm out and felt around to see where he was, expecting to find his arm by me. But he was asleep on the opposite side of that arm, lying on his stomach, facing the other way. It was my late maternal grandmother. When I had a CT scan on my heart in my late thirties, it involved doctors administering me with a medication which sped up my heart to

160+ beats per minute. As I lay there alone, trying not to gag, I felt a pressure on my forehead, which released when the ordeal was over. Nanny again.

On another occasion I was standing in the bathroom cleaning my teeth and felt a pressure in the middle of my back. This time the sensation wasn't like the one of my nan's hand on my wrist, which felt like it was a real human. But it was a distinct pressure. It was my paternal grandfather coming to say, 'Hi'.

These sensations occur when the energetic connection is so strong it feels like physical touch. On many occasions during meditation, I've felt an energy so strong around my hands, I know someone, most of the time, Quentin, is holding my hands. This happens as I lie in bed falling asleep sometimes and when meditating; it's either my guide or one of my loved ones.

One evening, sometime after Sam had moved out and I was finding life as a working single mum a bit overwhelming, I lay in bed and had the sensation of having my hands held. It was so intense I felt quite awestruck. It was more intense than I'd ever experienced. There was no other way of explaining it. I lay there marvelling at this beautiful warming, comforting, loving sensation, pure light energy. Pearl had long since died at this point, so I had to trust Quentin when he told me that it was Jesus holding my hands.

And then there are scents and sounds. I've smelt cigarette smoke and perfume which is there, so strong one minute, then gone the next. On a particularly vivid occasion, I was upstairs and the scent of woodsmoke was so strong I thought Sam had lit our wood burner in the lounge downstairs, which we hadn't done in about three years since Sonny was born. He hadn't. It lasted a good couple of minutes, the longest a scent had lingered around me before.

Often sounds come in the middle of the night. Why do things go bump in the night? It's when we're our most lucid, our most relaxed. It may be that there's an earthbound spirit passing through wanting to make itself known, or one of your loved ones who just want to say hello.

I've heard the doorbell go, but rather than it sounding like it came from downstairs, it was like it was in the room. I've heard knocks, like a rapping on the door. A dog bark, as if in the room; my paternal grandmother. And an enthusiastic 'Hello', which was weirdly in Sam's voice. We'd separated at this point and he'd moved out so I knew it wasn't him. It was my paternal grandmother again; she purposefully used Sam's voice so as not to scare me.

I know when it's my maternal grandmother letting me know she's around. For some reason she likes to make this rustling noise in my bedroom in the middle of the night. One time, it came from underneath my bed by the wall. It woke me up and I was wide awake listening to this noise, convinced it was a mouse until I came to and realised it was her letting me know she was around, again.

The first place we rented in Bristol was a simple three-bedroom semi-detached house, located in a quiet residential suburb on the city's southern fringe. But it wasn't long after moving in that I started to get a horrible feeling at the top of the stairs.

Quentin told me that someone had been hanged in this spot many years before. I consulted Pearl, and she agreed that even though the house hadn't been built when it happened, the height of the second stair down would have been about the height at which the person died.

I made a cross out of dried flowers, lifted up the floorboards and left it there, saying a prayer for them and urging them to go to the light. The bad feeling soon went. We'd completely forgotten about it when one day, a builder had cause to lift up the floorboards and found it. We heard him say, 'That's a bit weird'. Naturally, we denied all knowledge, feigning surprise.

Seeing spirits with your own eyes is obviously the most dramatic way of experiencing spirit. But, when you see them clearly in your mind's eye, these experiences are pretty impactful and unforgettable, too.

On one occasion in my early twenties, I'd been out kayaking on the River Dart on Dartmoor with friends, and sometime after falling asleep in my tent later that night, I was awoken. At first I thought I was still dreaming, as my eyes were closed. The vision I was experiencing was like a very vivid dream. In my mind's eye, I could see, as clear-as-day, a vision of a mother and daughter. The sadness in their eyes moved me to tears as they sat there looking right at me. The mother and daughter had drowned in the river. I prayed for them, for them to find peace and move on. Having had their passing acknowledged, they felt able to move on.

These sorts of mind's eye visions are the hardest to explain. But, once you've experienced one, they are very discernible from your imagination or dreams and feel resolutely real. One night, again in my early twenties, I was lying in bed, and the late father of a boyfriend I'd been with for almost a year, came to visit me. I woke up, startled, having sensed a presence in my room, and over by my wardrobe I saw his dad's face. Then, suddenly, his face was in front of mine, just a few inches away, smiling at me pleasantly. It was a vision, but I saw it with my eyes, not my mind's eye.

What was odd – as if the whole thing wasn't odd enough – was that he had a beard, though he never had one on the earth plane. Pearl told me when I rang her the next day that he'd presented himself with a beard to look more like my boyfriend, who did have one. He had come to tell me there would be no hard feelings if I finished with his son, which I'd been wanting to for a while, and did so a few weeks later.

Pearl was so down to earth, she brought authenticity to everything I was experiencing, which was a particular comfort at the times when I wondered whether labelling all my experiences as spirit-related was misguided and in fact I was just hallucinating. She kept me grounded, especially when it came to dealing with evil entities with the use of orbs, balls of light that I would telepathically trap them in.

As I developed and became a stronger medium, hearing my guides better and generally becoming more psychic, the dark side of the spirit realm also made itself known more. Because of the apparently important work I was here to do on the earth plane, the dark forces were aware of this and plagued me because they wanted to distract me and hinder my path, and generally annoy me. They succeeded at times. But not for long.

CHAPTER 14

ORBS

The power of the Lord's Prayer and of the cross should not be underestimated. Both keep evil and mischievous spirits at bay. Pearl told me how she had put evil spirits in 'balls' and got rid of them. This takes concentration and visualisation (telepathy) with your third eye.

During my first year of university, I'd returned home to my mum's house in Exmouth for the Easter holidays and was dropping off to sleep when I became aware of an extremely oppressive force around me. It became increasingly oppressive, and unmistakably evil. I knew it was the devil, come to exert his will over me, to warn me off, to frighten me. In my mind's eye he was a formidable, towering, black shadow.

But it didn't work. That evening, I said – told him – the Lord's Prayer. My rendition had immense conviction. I knew, in my whole being, that no matter what he threw at me, or the human race, the animal kingdom, or the planet, and no matter how much evil he tried to wield upon us, he would never, ever succeed. He will never win. Because, love trumps evil, and the force of good, the force of God, is more powerful than he'll ever be. And, actually, God lets him exist. This I told him too. I don't think he liked it much. Light will always overcome darkness.

Since then, I've gone up against him a few times. But while he tried to taunt me, I taunted him back. I've told him again and again that the only reason he exists is because God lets him exist, wants him to exist even, and that he is completely subservient to God's glory. He bothers me when I'm at my weakest, stressed about work or some other thing. That's when he rears his ugly head again, and when he either comes to bother me, or sends his nasty little minions out to annoy me instead.

The last time Satan bothered me was some time ago now. Gleefully, I told him I was going to get rid of him once and for all, and using the power of telepathy and psychic strength, I held him up in a ball in front of his armies of evil spirits amassing in his dimension, and told them all, 'If I can do this to your boss, don't even try to bother me.'

I've literally wiped-out hundreds of his minions. Those creations I do catch, I put in balls and send them off to other dimensions where they can't be reached and can never return, where they float in nothing. Essentially, I snuff them out of existence. But the devil keeps creating them.

I know when they're about because they put horrible thoughts in my head. They are sneaky now, whereas they used to be more blatant. When I'm busy, it's hard to find the time to get rid of them, but my guards are wise to them now so keep them at bay, and reciting the Lord's Prayer to them with conviction is always a sure-fire way of warding them off.

When I was talking to Pearl about healing one day, Brother Joseph said I was a healer, one whose means of healing is through words. As an empath, I'd always found myself listening to people's problems and trying to make them feel better by talking things through with them and giving advice. I used to love being an 'agony aunt' as a teenager. The older I got I realised what I said actually worked, and my friends felt better after talking to me. So when she said this, it made sense why people were drawn to me, opened up and confided in me.

I didn't make the connection at time, but I later figured that this was why I was drawn to journalism, and particularly telling people's stories, giving people a voice and challenging injustices. I always hoped that my stories would have an impact. At the very least, I hoped that some of the thousands of news stories I'd written over the years helped people feel better, having been given the platform to share their experiences and be heard.

Pearl, on the other hand was a hands-on spiritual healer. Spiritual healing can achieve something more profound than prayer and the more powerful the medium, the more effective the healing.

In my thirties I turned to Reiki, energy healing, whereby you draw upon the energy within you and around you and channel that into the person or animal who needs healing. At the same time, I say a prayer because this energy comes from Source, or God. Reiki became part of my everyday existence, intertwined with my long held spiritual beliefs, ever since. I learnt to use the power of visualisation to heal and protect. And I learnt how important it was to ensure my own light was shining as bright as it could be, in order to give light to others in need.

During my Reiki one course, my teacher, a life-long medium and Christian, brought our focus to the energy coursing through us, bringing our attention to the vibration in the palms of our hands. She introduced us to the energy within essential oils and crystals. She asked us to choose a crystal, the one we were most drawn to, and hold it in the palm of our right hand, then stand, feet shoulder width apart, eyes closed. We found we were either ever so slightly pulled forwards or backwards. The same happened when we held a bottle of essential oil to our heart chakra. Being pulled forwards means the item you're holding is right for you, being pulled backwards means it's not.

Then she demonstrated divination using dowsing rods, fashioned out of a coat hanger. The exercise was to show how the rods reacted to the energy stored in our bodies. Starting at the top, as she held them over my head, they swung out a little, indicating that there was a strong energetic vibration there. As she moved down my torso to my reproductive system, they waved all over the place. This made us, and the other lady on the course, laugh a lot, given that I was newly single!

For the other lady on the course, the rods waved about in the area of her heart chakra, indicating there was emotional energy being stored there that she needed to release.

When I came to give our teacher Reiki, I took deep breaths, visualising light and energy around me and within me, flowing along my arms and through my fingertips into her body. You are guided to where the energy is needed most. And, for some reason, I was guided to her ankles. Afterwards she told me she had been experiencing pain in her ankle joints for several months. I was pretty chuffed! And it gave me confidence.

Such was the busyness of life, since my Reiki one and two courses, I rarely practised energy healing in the traditional sense whereby someone lies down in front of you in real life. Instead, I started doing it telepathically, sometimes closing my eyes and visualising the energy being sent to a certain person. Other times,

I'd do it to random passers-by in the street if I sensed they needed a pick-me-up.

There were also times that I lay on my bedroom floor on a Friday night and visualised pushing back against Putin's bombs which he was sending to Ukraine.

Sending positive healing energy out is something within all of our power, and is a way we can all help others in need and the world at large.

CHAPTER 15
NIBAA

THE HISTORY OF THE FIRST Nations people in North America has been tumultuous; ever since European settlers arrived in the 1400s they've endured a trajectory of violence and oppression, discrimination and poverty.

In Canada there are 634 First Nations governments, 45 in Alberta. The term 'Red Indian' was bestowed upon the continent's indigenous people by European invaders and is therefore derogatory and shouldn't be used. Further south, the United States' indigenous people are known as Native Americans.

When the Europeans arrived, they set about forcibly removing the indigenous people from their ancestral lands, enforcing their own governmental system and law of order and rule. This was a time of war and extreme violence on both sides. The traditions and way of life of the indigenous peoples was desecrated, never to be the same again.

Then, between the late 1700s and early 1900s, indigenous peoples were subjected to forced cultural assimilation, with a rule book called the Indian Act imposed upon First Nations people and passed in 1876 to consolidate existing laws regarding their rights. The act had the effect of homogenising a culturally diverse people, restricting their expression and cultural identity. Religious and cultural practices like their powwows and sacred sun dance were banned. In this way it was an oppressive and coercive method of governance. Many amendments have occurred over the years with the contemporary version outlining the terms of their status and reserves.

In January 2023, the BBC reported that the Canadian government agreed to pay C$2.8bn to settle a class-action lawsuit 'seeking compensation for the loss of language and culture caused by its residential school system': during the 1900s up until the 1970s, around 150,000 First Nations, Métis and Inuit children were taken from their families and placed in government boarding schools, as part of an assimilation policy to destroy indigenous cultures and languages. The BBC report stated that the lawsuit was brought by 325 First Nations in 2012 and sought reparations for the abuse indigenous Canadians faced at government boarding schools.

We stocked up on provisions and made an inventory of items we'd need to be able to live off the land, should we need to. Then, we headed north on Highway 35 and then west along Highway 58 to Rainbow Lake.

It was late afternoon by the time we arrived in this hidden crease in the hills which was to be our home for eleven weeks. We arrived at what looked like a pop-up village of campers, trucks and trailers of varying sizes, all occupied by Canadians, including First Nations.

As the residents spotted us pulling into camp, they shot us big, knowing, smiles. We smiled back and exited our truck to a warm welcome of hugs and offers of tea and supper.

'I'm here to throw stones in your cosmic greenhouse.' This was the first thing Nibaa said to me.

He was one of the first people we met at the lake. Sonny and Marnie had gone to bed. Most people had when I first saw him. A solitude silhouette against the glowing embers of the lakeside fire. Tall, with dark brown hair in a nineties-boyband curtains style, and a nose ring, Nib was a young-at-heart fifty-three-year-old from the Lil'wat Nation community near Pemberton, British Columbia, two hours north of Vancouver. When he turned around and shot me a smile, eyes sparkling, I felt a sudden rush of energy surge up my torso, through my heart and lungs, to the crown of my head and down my arms into my hands and fingers which began buzzing with the exact same feeling I got when I did Reiki.

Our connection was instantaneous and puzzling. The attraction raw and inexplicable. He and three friends were among the first residents to arrive at the lake almost five weeks previously and they had been integral in setting up the site to accommodate up to one hundred more people if necessary, fixing compost toilets and constructing a sheltered outdoor kitchen and lounge area, furnished with items salvaged from Peace River's recycling centre.

'It's a work in progress,' he told me another time.

In his twenties, when he was working as a carpenter, Nib found himself developing shamanically. He found it easy to go into trance and began soul journeying, assisting with exorcisms of properties and psychopomp; guiding lost souls over to the Other Side.

As the campfire kept us warm late into the night, he told me about his most, 'amazing ever experience'...

🌰

Looking back, I got the call from spirit to hit the road on some grand old adventure at the exact same time that Big Tim rang me out of the blue, suggesting that I jump on a plane and cross the Atlantic to visit him in Europe without planning or delay. He told me it would reconnect me with my 'medicine' and get me out of the ditch he knew I'd been in. I mean, just because you think you're some all-seeing shaman, doesn't mean that you can avoid those devilish blues or that you're too damned big to receive the right sort of help. I didn't realise then just how profound and life-changing that journey would turn out to be.

On the flight over I started to cringe about allowing myself to be rescued, then became more and more sceptical about what Tim was espousing – a *soirée* to the Bosnian Pyramid Valley. It all sounded too much like one of those classic buddy-up road trips, to see something strange in some far-flung place that probably wouldn't amount to much in the end.

But as it turned out the destination was pretty unique, way down in the Balkans, not that I knew where that was. Big Tim announced it bombastically during our initial call as if trying to fish hook me into making the decision to go. I was instantly curious of course, I have to admit, but I saw it as nothing more than some time-out with some good company in a strange land where we'd sink a few beers and soothe our souls.

But I soon discovered that I'd majorly underestimated my old alchemical friend. It happened from time to time over the thirty years we'd been locking spiritual horns. And as it turned out I returned to Canada, completely renewed and refreshed in every sort of sense. And in Tim's own immortal words, 'You never regret stepping onto some magic carpet ride!'

Tim was a science man, part-time alchemist and potion-maker extraordinaire. He was well-known in his city in Germany and further afield, respected on the alternative scene for quite some years. But I was still mighty unsure about going, even after booking that flight, deciding in the end to just trust his crazy-sounding plan and take the plunge. For Tim knew a thing or two about pyramids, that much was clear, and not just the ones you found down in Giza, but ones that were bigger and older and standing twice as high, up in Bosnia-Herzegovina.

Not long after I touched down in Germany, we loaded up his old silver Mercedes and drove south east to Croatia before losing ourselves in the green and rugged terrain of mineral-rich Bosnia. When we arrived, the former Yugoslavia seemed to welcome us with a mystical embrace, Tim insisting still that something truly special awaited us that would seriously reset my soul.

After a restorative first night's sleep in that strange and mysterious land, in the beguiling city of Sarajevo in some back-street hotel, my feelings started to really change. I started to get a growing sense deep in my bones that it was going to be more than an esoteric tap on the nose and that something special was brewing in those foothills around Visoko, where the mist-shrouded pyramids were lying in wait.

So, excitedly, we took a taxi early the next morning from the capital to that modest yet ancient town, where approximately forty thousand people now lived and thrived, nestled on a flood plain where two powerful rivers met, in the shadow of some impressive looking hills, clad in a cloak of dense emerald forest.

On arrival, we headed straight for the main entrance of the Ravne Tunnels where we hurriedly bought tickets and joined a group of explorers readying themselves to go in. As we shuffled to the door I overheard one of them say that the tunnels fanned out for miles underneath the entire valley. I swallowed with trepidation. Hard hats and torches at the ready, we were heading in!

As the narrow low-lit tunnels slowly swallowed us up, Tim announced that we were entering them on the shoulder of the 'Pyramid of the Sun', which was the biggest and most impressive of the seven pyramids that had been discovered, and that people experienced strange things down there; people had reported seeing flying lights and feeling unearthly tremors, others claimed to have undergone huge transformations in both their physical health and their psychic development as a result of their visits.

'It's all down to the negative ions,' Big Tim insisted, with one of his all-knowing smiles; the conditions were on par with what you'd find in some Tibetan temple or wild mountain terrain. Archaeologists had detected the powerful Schumann resonance down there too of 7.38 hertz, known as the mysterious heartbeat of the Earth which helped the body return to its optimum vibration.

Of course, as I entered, I thought it just looked like some abandoned old tin mine. But after a few hundred yards I realised that there really was something going on that couldn't be ignored – this place had an unspoken power, a presence about it that enveloped you more and more the further you went in, like some huge cosmic bear!

Instinctively and stealthily, I slowly hung back from the rest of the group until after a while all I could hear were whispering voices and the echoes of their shuffling feet. We were going in deeper now and it was darker and colder too. I felt an insistence that I commune with this place alone in the dark, that somehow I should bare my soul.

I took another path and carried on walking for what felt like an age, before arriving into a chamber with some shadowy object at its centre, like some sacrificial beast that had been awaiting my arrival. I skimmed my flashlight across the stone-packed walls, then across the dirt floor of this liminal space, before settling on a huge man-made boulder that I felt had called me in.

I knelt down in reverence and ran a hand over its surface. It felt cool and ceramic, and radiant with some tangible force. Tim had said that scientists had found quartz crystals set within its artificial core too, and that many believed the stone was some ancient and spiritual machine.

For a second, I just stared at the thing deep in awe, like some washed up walrus on a windswept shore, not sure what to do next before instinctively closing my eyes and rocking myself shamanically to tune into its mass.

These pyramids were over thirty-thousand years old, and some people had created that boulder way back when, in the earliest of days when we were told humans were just wandering around in furs and living in caves. Yet somehow, someone had managed to bring that massive thing down the narrowest of passages and into this chamber, and the more I thought about it, the more it just blew my mind!

And now, as I sat deep in the belly of the all-embracing mother, in tunnels crafted long ago by ancient and skilled hands, a thumping silence began to pulse and pound my ears. In the shapeshifting shadows it seemed as if ancestral eyes were observing and animals were circling, that some ancient guardian was compelling me to lie down with this strange stone.

So, I lowered myself down and pressed myself tightly in, then let my mind go blank and started to hum until I felt my spirit soar. Quickly I felt my energy pulse and flow with the rock's ancient song, and that's when it happened, in almost a flash and with a boom, a journey to that incredible world, a place that felt so familiar but where I'd never travelled spiritually before.

I decided to trust and let myself fall deeper into some otherworldly shaft of prismatic light with lilacs and magentas and deep purples that just seemed to tornado around my astral body as each second passed – the heaviness of my life seemingly energetically cleansed.

Then, much to my relief, I finally landed at its end, and found myself sitting in some celestial pool, where I opened my eyes to see where I'd been taken. And to my shock and disbelief I couldn't believe what lay above, before and around me. I was sat staring up at some vast cavern so big that there was some futuristic city resting inside – yes, a city, and it was breathtaking in size and design!

I stared in disbelief, rooted to the spot. There were hundreds of triangular and mushroom-shaped buildings made of crystal or glass, and flying cars disappearing into high-rise buildings that melted into the darkness above. The whole place seemed illuminated by some strange plasma impregnated into the rock. Endless forests glowed and bustled with life and long-extinct animals that appeared to roam freely.

I stood up and stepped out of the pool and then wandered around cautiously, still in a daze. There were other humans down there too, who were similar to me and walking around freely, but they were taller and more luminous and dressed in otherworldly robes in a variety of colours.

As I passed them, they looked upon me with unspoken care, filling me with a greater sense of ease. Here, it seemed, civilisation was more evolved and advanced, peaceful and kind, encouraging me to explore more of this mystical Shamballa.

So, I headed towards the nearest mushroom-shaped building and from its lobby took an elevator up to the top, where sliding doors opened out onto a white circular room offering a panoramic view, where a group of benevolent beings beckoned me to lie down on a couch made of crystal, positioned in its centre.

A woman with presence stepped forward and bid me to close my eyes. Immediately, coloured lights shot and whirled into my mind and my energetic body pulsed and hummed – information was being downloaded, blockages cleared and emotions transmuted, and the woman started to speak to me without words, saying, 'All will be well, Nib, we have been ready and waiting for some time. Your body will become lighter and your senses will expand.'

It was as if I was being worked on, in some fifth dimensional surgery, in what felt like the centre of the Earth. It was all truly extraordinary as it felt so extraordinarily real. For a moment I took a deep breath as realisation sunk further in – these Shamballa people, who had been written about and spoken of through the ages, truly existed, and now I was lucky enough to have been gifted a front row seat.

When I woke up, I was back on my bed in my hotel on the outskirts of Sarajevo. Tim was sat on the bed opposite grinning at me boyishly like he did when he knew he was right.

'What happened?' I asked groggily.

'You staggered out the tunnels about half-an-hour later, then just passed out right outside the main entrance, Nib.'

Tim's words were etched with joy as much as they were with concern.

'These Pyramids are some sort of portal, Tim, but you knew that right?' I said.

He looked at me intensely.

'Yes, I did, Nib.'

'I mean, there are flying cars down there man, and crystal cities built in vast illuminated caverns,' I went on. 'I went there astrally, Tim, and I know it exists. This wasn't just another journey to another dimension to find some shard of soul – this was a visit to the centre of the Earth!'

Big Tim flashed another one of his all-knowing smiles.

'I knew that they would let you in, but not everyone is,' he replied. 'That place is heavily protected, and for obvious reasons. The energy in some of those boulders is so strong that it can take you to another level, Nib, if you're ready and willing – they hold a frequency that vibrates with the inner world, allowing you to harmonise with it and then travel down there, out of your body.'

'It's hard to wrap your head around it,' I said sitting up in bed.

'Now you're connected, they will link up with you at will, they'll start working with you, I'm sure.'

As if on cue, a darting light caught the periphery of my vision and made me glance to my right. In the half-light of the dimly-lit room I could see clearly one of those beings again, standing there in translucent robes looking almost like some Atlantean wizard. He exuded a deep calm and wisdom that just seemed to wash over my body and into my mind.

'You have much work to do, my child,' he said. 'You have climbed a spiritual mountain of which we are proud, but another challenge awaits, which we will guide you through step by step.'

I blew out the breath I'd been holding onto then felt warm powerful energy course through my body again.

'The beings of the inner world stand gently at your side now, Nib, as do your loved ones – for a great cycle has ended and a new one is about to begin. And we will help you write about our existence in plain language and with passion, so that everyone can hear and understand our song.'

I went to say something but in the blink of an eye the white-robed figure was gone.

'Tell people about us, Nib, let them hear our calling,' I heard him whisper, as he started to fade. 'Let them read about us...Let them activate their higher minds...For the inner earth welcomes all those who can walk in peace, who can speak with their heart, who have courage to walk the sacred path.'

CHAPTER 16

READINGS

It was 2005 when Sam and I moved back to the UK from Canada. New to Bristol, we wanted to meet other spiritually minded people and decided to experience what a spiritualist church was like. The spiritualist movement has churches all over the place and their meetings are universal in their format.

One of the loveliest aspects about these meetings is that the congregation spend one minute sending healing to the world, directing it to where it's most needed, as perceived by the sender. There's also prayer, a sermon by the church leader and a thought-provoking talk from a visiting medium. The final element is the demonstration of mediumship. This is when the visiting medium gives messages from spirit to members of the congregation.

While all platform mediums work in different ways, the majority of those I've seen look into the audience and almost immediately know who they want to talk to. The messages pretty much always start with a confirmation, so information specific to the intended recipient will be given to the medium by whoever is in spirit coming through to them, be it a family member, a friend, or the medium's spirit guide. This makes the connection with the recipient, and also, if there was any doubt, provides credibility.

In the majority of instances I've witnessed over the years, the recipient recognises those in spirit giving the message to them from the Other Side.

In Bristol, there were several spiritualist groups which met once a week on a Sunday evening. Sam and I found one in Clifton, the closest one to where we lived south of the river, and, excuse the cliché, but it really was like 'coming home'. Located at a Quaker meeting house, the congregation fluctuated between a handful of regulars and a congregation of around twenty on some occasions, filling all of the available chairs.

We received the most beautiful messages from family members and friends who were in spirit, but also from the many helpers we all have, for varying durations, all who have our back.

And yes, even mediums like to receive messages from spirit via other mediums!

Who the medium goes to is determined by spirit, so it can often depend on how strident our loved ones are jostling for position.

Sometimes, a medium is not sure about who the recipient of an impending message is, so the medium will say, for example, 'I have a gentleman standing with me, he's giving me the initial 'J', does that mean anything to anyone?' And if it does, members of the audience are encouraged to put their hands up, and as the message continues, by process of elimination, the intended recipient of the message is revealed.

Even if you don't receive a message at these meetings, or indeed if you've bought a ticket to go and see a medium on stage for entertainment, you are encouraged to take what you can from the messages given to others because they are full of generic insights and words of wisdom that often apply to us all, therefore inspiring a more enlightened perspective and hopefully a greater sense of well-being.

Certain themes and messages come up again and again: trusting your gut instinct, that feeling of knowing deep within you, is an important one, for this is spirit's way of communicating with us. This is how we can know the truth in a situation. The answers we seek are within us.

Also, trusting in the 'small signs', the seemingly insignificant, inconspicuous signs around us which are the ways our loved ones communicate with us and give us a nudge in the right direction, like a song coming on the radio which really resonates with you at that particular time. The more attention you pay to the little things, the more you'll be able to discern the difference between your imagination and what has been given to you from spirit, until you get to a point where you just know.

They also like reminding us that our lives here on Earth are all about learning, growing, developing and reaching enlightenment. And while we can reflect on the past to better our lives now, and in the future, we should never look back and dwell on the past, just learn from it.

Another message which kept coming up over the years was how the Other Side want us to ask for help: asking opens up the channel between us and the spirit realm making it easier for them to help. They are all poised waiting, wanting to help us.

Because our group was usually so small in Bristol, often all of us would receive a message each week. Irrespective that communicating with the spirit world was normal for me, there was a novelty to every message I received. Each one, regardless of who the visiting medium was, was incredibly moving and beautiful.

When Sam and I started going to the meetings, I was going through a particularly challenging period in my life circumstantially and therefore emotionally and psychologically. The mediums all picked up on this and the impetus of their messages revolved around bringing me love and support.

I documented the majority of my readings over the years; the most poignant parts are included here. Although the messages are specific to me, I have selected the parts of the readings with insights for us all, to demonstrate that we are all being looked after by those in spirit.

EARLY READINGS

TED

One of the first readings I received was from a medium called Ted. He started by asking me if I was an artist; I went to art college for a year between school and university. He went on to say I needed some solitude, 'I feel like I want to put you in a bubble', he said.

He asked if January was a significant month to me; my maternal grandfather died in January. Then he asked me if I'd ever hurt an ankle; during my second year of university, I was waiting outside a city centre nightclub and a woman drove over my foot in her car and then sped off. Her passenger side front wheel went over my foot in such a way it caused my ankle to twist, and although it didn't break, it was sprained so badly I could hardly put weight on it for about two months.

He said that my maternal grandmother was giving me bracelets, and, putting a wedding ring on my finger. Sam and I got married a year or so later. He asked me if I'd ever received a ring from her; it was in a trinket box of keepsakes somewhere. He said she wanted me to wear it to remind me she was close. That evening, I dug it out and put it on.

He said spirit wanted to give me roses and dahlias, continuing, 'I'm sensing a lot of sadness with you.'

Ted ended the reading by holding my hands and rubbing them with imaginary gold dust.

Another evening, a different medium said she felt like giving a 'big sigh', getting the sense I was 'fed up'. She said there was an opportunity out there waiting to happen and that spirit wanted it to happen. She said I'd be doing something completely different and gave a timescale of six months. She told me to listen to my guide, because he was helping me.

Another medium said she felt like I was waiting for something 'with nervous anticipation'. She said that on the outside, I get on with things, but it's always there, affecting my health, affecting my sleep. She said it would get worse if I didn't 'shelve it'.

By this she meant that we need to 'hand our problems over to spirit to deal with'. Let them take the burden from you and trust that they will help sort things out with you. She added, 'What you're waiting for is imminent, so, until then, give things to God to look after.'

They were right in seeing change afoot.

CATHERINE

Catherine said she had a lady in spirit, one of my helpers, telling me that I had a light shining around me. She said, 'Even if you don't know it, the kindness shines out.' She said I had a lot to be thankful for, 'So don't feel hard done by.' This jolted me into always 'look on the bright side of life', a sentiment we should all strive to live by to feel greater contentment.

She said she had a man and a woman with her, and two 'little ones', a girl and a boy, bringing me love. And a spotty dog, by my feet, also bringing me love. I didn't recognise any of them. But we have a lot of people helping us in spirit that we don't know.

She asked if I read a lot, because she saw lots of books around me. And she asked me if I was studying. I wasn't, but I was writing a lot. Whenever I wasn't working, I was writing. They don't always get things entirely correct!

RITA

Rita asked me whether my hands ever tingled. I said they did, and she said, 'When they do, send a prayer out to someone.' She asked me if I ever sent out absent healing. I tried, I replied, and she said, 'Well, it's working, keep doing it.'

She said she had a sense of being far, far away around the world. I mentioned that Sam was Canadian and we'd met there. She said she saw us at an airport and that he should visit his mum because she got the feeling that she needed his love. She added, 'We never know how long we've got here.'

JOAN

On another occasion, my maternal grandmother came through with flowers of different healing colours. Joan went on to ask if gardens meant anything to me and then passed on a vision of a garden with a swing in it. She said the Other Side wanted to bring joy back into my life, a joy that had been 'missing for so long'.

She recognised that I take on other people's problems, adding that everyone is responsible for their own lives, and that, while empathy is good, it can also mean you become overwhelmed when you're very sensitive and pick up on other people's energy. She told me that I needed to be around natural spaces to rejuvenate and asked me if I walked in water. This made me laugh. In the summer months as well as floating and swimming, I'd often walk around on the seabed as well, enjoying the feeling of it!

She got a sense of me 'not knowing where to turn', like being a rabbit in the headlights. And she told me to step outside the box and close the lid. I didn't know what this meant but that evening as I pondered over the message I realised they wanted me to move on and leave it all behind me.

She got the sense of dancing, and, again, told us to bring the joy back into our lives. This is important – we are meant to be happy and spirit want this for us.

She said Sam and I didn't spend enough time together. Then, my maternal grandparents came through and put a heart around us and gave us each a bouquet of flowers. She finished by telling me that my head doesn't know which way to turn, and in my dreams, I try and interpret things. Spiritual work goes on at night in our subconscious, even if we don't know it.

HANNAH

'You've had a lot of things thrown at you, a lot to deal with recently,' She began. 'Sometimes you feel like giving up. You're a survivor, you keep going. You're getting stronger.

'Do butterflies mean anything to you? You are like a butterfly, coming out of a chrysalis, this is you coming into your own persona. There is someone behind you, an aunt, holding you up, they are pushing you on. I'm being shown biscuit tins – are you looking for something?

'I'm being shown a cupboard full of jars – your nan is saying there is better use for it! This is symbolic of your state of mind.' This made us laugh. I was indeed storing jars in case I ever needed one, and had a whole cupboard dedicated to them! They all went out in the recycling the next day.

She added: 'Does the name Tom mean anything to you?' My friend Tom from university had died eighteen months prior.

'Your nan is saying that she is trying to lift the weight from your shoulders. She is giving you some lavender sprigs. She says you bear the weight of other people's problems and you should pass them onto spirit to take care of.

'She is coming in with a pack of cards. She wants to bring the fun back into your life. She's dealing them out, saying. "What's going to happen, what's each one going to be...?"' I grew up playing cards with her and still have the pack we played with.

'She is giving you love and healing energy.

'Are you moving?' She went off on a tangent. 'You will be. Start preparing.'

DANIEL

About a month before I got my job on a regional newspaper in Devon and we moved out of Bristol, I was at the lowest point I'd ever been in my life. But during this time I'd discovered writing as a hobby. Whenever I had a spare moment I would write, including short stories about our adventurous activities as well as music reviews and other musings, for a free independent pocket magazine distributed around the city.

I knew from my own guide that I should keep writing, but such was my state of mind at this point in my life, I sought guidance from other mediums, for they can help with insight which is at times not possible to find yourself, for yourself.

So, I booked in for a reading with a trance medium called Daniel, a member of the spiritualist church congregation. Daniel was in his early thirties and was soon to move to Cornwall with his wife. Trance mediums are able to let a spirit take over their bodies and voices. So, spirit speaks through them. Despite all my own spiritual encounters, the hour I spent with Daniel remains one of the most amazing experiences I've ever had.

'A lady has come through with a lovely smile and rosy cheeks,' he began. 'She's telling me you are wrestling with many sides; there are lots of sides to you which need fulfilment.

'She keeps calling you "dear". She's brought you an apple. You carry the world on your shoulders. She is bringing you lavender to calm you down.

'Someone who is very gentle and softly spoken is bringing you Jammy Dodgers to bring the sweetness back into your life.' I didn't like Jammy Dodgers. They were Sam's favourite biscuits. So while they could have chosen any biscuit to illustrate this point, they chose these to forge a connection with me and offer a little proof that they are watching over us.

'Does the number fourteen mean anything to you?' Number 14 was our house number. 'You're not meant to be here. You're being pushed out of Bristol. This is why doors are closing in your face.' This was a powerful moment because many doors had closed and there had been a distinct lack of positive experiences over the previous four years for both myself and Sam.

'You need to be near water,' Daniel continued. 'Your nan is showing me a crib board and dominoes. You need to play more games. She's also saying that there will be more guineas in the pot.'

My maternal grandfather came through at this point.

Daniel continued, 'He's telling me to "Sit up straight boy!" He was one who liked to have a joke! He's showing me a carousel; you have lots of ideas and thoughts going around in your head, but the only thing that should be going around is a carousel, at least that's more fun!'

Daniel picked four cards: creative writing, clear your space, clairsentience and beloved one (which means help with spiritual soulmate relationships).

At this point, Daniel went into a trance. The first person to come though was an African man, John, Daniel's guide. The next bit is what John said, through Daniel, who had his eyes shut the whole time and suddenly had a distinctly lower voice as well as a different physical stature and different mannerisms.

'We're delighted to see you,' John said. 'We see you as a flower. You need sunlight to grow and nighttime to rest.

'Life is like the tides of the sea and the seasons. You are learning. You need to go through these things. You will be stronger for it.

Don't be troubled by those who shout at you, for they are suffering too. Show love to others.

'When the tide is right, there will be opportunity. They're putting things in place for opportunities to happen.'

Daniel came out of the trance and very quickly went into another. He told me afterwards that only once before had he gone into trance twice in a reading. They must really have wanted me to listen!

This time it was an African-American man. I don't know the significance of why he came through to me, but Daniel said he was one of my helpers, to help me with 'toiling in the fields and fulfilling my passions'.

'It's wonderful to have you here,' he said. 'Watch the way the moon works. All women are governed by her.

'We've come to uplift you. I toiled in the fields in the day and let my hair down in the evening. I loved the Blues. I know my passions are different to yours. You are toiling in the fields too.' He added, 'There's to be no more self-doubt.'

A Romany Gypsy fortune teller came through to Daniel reading the tea leaves and brandishing a crystal ball. She showed him that 'the clouds are passing' and that she could see my name in print next to articles.

A few weeks later, over Easter, I did work experience on the newspaper in Exeter. A few weeks after that, the editor phoned me up and offered me a job. So that's when we moved to Devon. Indeed, my byline has been on thousands of news articles and features ever since.

LATER READINGS

Throughout my thirties, I had readings with four very good mediums. Their shared prowess was in knowing the precise nature of my circumstances and my state of mind at the time of the reading, and their awareness of events and people who had played a significant part in my life. They knew, without me saying a word, what guidance I needed.

I never asked my guides what was coming up, simply because I don't think it's a healthy way to live, nor is it wise to invest too much energy in the predictions a medium makes, because there are so many variables, particularly other people. And spirit only 'know' the future based on the present, so things can change.

Over a decade, during which time Sam and I separated and I became a single mum (while applying for the aforementioned series of jobs), because stress was blocking my intuition, it was clarity and guidance I sought from these other mediums.

When you go for a reading, mediums prefer you give nothing away at first so they know what they're hearing is authentic and is exactly what spirit wants you to know, free from any influences. I have never had a reading with the purpose of finding out the future. But they will pass on what they are given by their guides, or anyone else who comes through to them in spirit, so inevitably they end up prophesising.

TAMSIN

The first time I had a reading with Tamsin, she was entirely accurate. She told me that a soul was waiting, ready to come in. Ten days later, after fourteen emotional months of trying for a baby, I conceived.

Shortly after I had Sonny, I had another reading with Tamsin, and she opened with, 'Mabel is sending you lots of love.' How lovely, I thought. But who is Mabel? 'She just wanted to say hello and well done on Sonny,' she continued.

'He's got some life in front of him,' she said. 'He's with the right parents. You'll have to be holding him back the whole time! As an adult, he's going to do really good work. Whatever it is he's going to do, it's going to benefit the whole world. His brain's ahead of himself already. He was very much wanted, wasn't he? He's very well protected. He's definitely got the parents he needs.'

She picked up on 'America'. Not the first medium to say so, and not the last.

Then my maternal grandfather came through, saying, 'You don't realise until you get over here how much women are expected to do.' Then he said, 'You don't ask spirit for enough help.'

Readings can jump around a fair bit, from one topic or thought, to the next.

Tamsin predicted a little girl on the way. This I was told by other mediums in the following years. I only ever had Sonny.

GWEN

The next reading I had was about a year later with a medium called Gwen, on the phone. She started the reading by telling me another child would come, but after a long wait.

The soulmate card came out three times in quick succession. But this wasn't reaffirming my relationship with Sam, rather, she, very frankly, said that our relationship was not going to last much longer, and that there were other soulmates out there for us both.

She told me we only came together to parent our son. We entered a 'soul contract'. And now, it was time to part. I knew this in my heart, but it was hard hearing this and this reading was hugely emotional. She picked up on the fact that Sam hadn't done anything wrong, just that things had just changed between us.

Gwen was the first of subsequent mediums who all said the same thing; that there would be a change in both living, work and relationship circumstances. She said Sam would cope 'just fine' with our separation. He did! She also predicted that I'd be working for myself in 'about five years' time'. I was!

She, like all the others, told me to listen to my intuition. She ended by saying, 'You've got to be true to yourself or you won't be able to fulfil what you're here to do. You can't get bogged down with the material stuff. If you're not happy, you're not on your proper pathway.'

The same themes of job changes, a new relationship, and things 'getting better' arose in readings again and again over the proceeding eight years. But what became clear, is that they really do have no perception of time in the spirit world!

Gwen was the second medium to say Sonny was a 'star child'. She asked if he had blue eyes and blond hair. He did. She said he'd always seem more advanced than his years, 'an old head on young shoulders.' At age eight, he was better at chess than me so this wasn't hard to believe!

'He'll be interested in the oceans, the stars and the planets. *Why* will be his main word. He draws people to him. He's here to make a difference and to challenge authority. You have to be careful about what you say, he's very sensitive. Even at his age he's open to energies. He's an empath. Not everyone is chosen to give birth to one,' Gwen told me.

I had another reading with her about nine months before mine and Sam's separation. She started by saying, 'There's going to be a change in accommodation. What a funny way of putting it, but that's what they're saying,' she mused. There was a change in accommodation – Sam moved out.

My maternal grandmother then came through and said, 'We have things thrown at us to test our mettle, to see what we're made of.'

Again, Gwen said they'd be a change across the board, the 'old life new life' card came out again; a change of job and change of relationship is coming, she asserted.

She said I was an empath and this needed to feed into my work. It did, I was pursuing investigative journalism at the time. She added that more money would come in. 'The more we put ourselves in service to others, the more renumeration we can expect,' she added.

At this point, I'd been freelance for almost four years and through working as a photographer for free for charities, I'd attracted well paid gigs.

'There's something out there that will suit you down to the ground. Don't make it fit. If it's not right, keep looking,' she said, in the midst of my mass job application stint.

The 'steps to success' card came out again on this reading. Unfortunately, she predicted, wrongly, that 'June, will be the time you breathe a sigh of relief'.

She did, however, pick up on the fact I felt unappreciated. 'Being unappreciated is the universe's way of getting us out of there,' she said. 'Follow your gut instinct and things will fall into place.'

She mentioned my impending soulmate again. 'Someone's going to pique your interest and you're not going to want to let him go. You can't miss him. It's like destiny waiting to happen.' I'm still waiting for said someone to pique my interest – and be available.

Again, she said Sonny was a 'diamond' or 'crystal' child. 'They're here to make a difference in the world,' she explained. 'They come to shake us up. They bring things to a head and make us look inside ourselves.'

She predicted a year of 'very good changes'. The only change that year was the separation. Whereas the Other Side's perception was that this was a 'good' change, it took me a while to view it as such. It is often the case that challenging incidents in life that we perceive as negative or bad are actually the opposite, and are opportunities or springboards to something better.

'Don't do what you ought to do, or what you think you should do,' she added. While on the earth plane, we often live our lives doing things we think we ought to do, not what we want to do. The Other Side want us to be our authentic selves, not try to be things we're not; that is when things will flow and work out for the best.'

Gwen said April, May and June were the months where things would take effect. 'A job is going to come in at the eleventh hour and help you out,' she asserted. She predicted a 'big pool of money' and pulled out the card of 'being in limbo but close to a breakthrough. You'll be in a position to buy yourself a house. By the end of the year you'll be in a much better place,' she offered. 'I think it's going to be an amazing year.'

As confirmation, at the end of the reading, she asked me if there was an issue with my car. There was. I'd booked it in for a new tyre that afternoon.

In fact, challenges continued to beset the months ahead, and these things didn't come to pass.

TAMSIN

I had another reading with Tamsin almost a year later. She said some wonderfully profound things.

'Stand still for a moment, do nothing, step back. If you don't, everything will be stopped around you anyway.'

By this point, I'd been doggedly applying for jobs all over the country for several years. Keeping my pecker up was difficult.

'I know each day you want to feel better, but it feels like you're rushing to get well,' she continued. 'What they're saying is that it will take time, but they need you to stop trying. Rushing through it isn't going to work.'

I quite enjoyed being told to do nothing. Doing everything was exhausting. It was this summer when I met the soulmate

Gwen had mentioned. It was a brief dalliance, but one which left me pretty wounded.

'I get the feeling someone's left you suddenly,' Tamsin said. 'I'm going to give you a warning – he is quite unsuitable, he has lots of underlying issues. He can turn very cold very quickly. He's a control freak and eventually he'll take over your life. Move on from him. He can be arrogant. He wouldn't be positive in your life. He's started to demonstrate behaviours already, that he's not all he's cracked up to be.' She was right. But this was a revelation to me that soulmates are not always connected with love and can actually be unpleasant encounters, and be very fleeting, and yet they play an important role in your development, helping you learn a lesson, learn about yourself, or move you along in your life.

She predicted a new job opportunity, one which would take me abroad and to London. This was around the time the coronavirus pandemic changed the world. There was no job opportunity. Instead, I found myself in a contract for the public sector for eighteen months!

Two years later, after setting up my own business, my main client was a company which worked ninety per cent overseas. I did get to work from home, but I didn't get to go on their overseas projects, and I never had cause to go to London. I figured this is what she saw for me, just in a slightly wonky way!

Moving on, she added, 'In your teens you felt different and separated, particularly at school. You enjoyed friends but felt detached from them. You looked at people's behaviours and struggled to understand them. And there was a disappointment there.' She absolutely nailed how I felt. It was a comfort to know that my interminable internal struggle with humanity was known by the Other Side! 'You chose a spiritual life in your teens,' she continued. 'You've got a gift of words and are very effective.'

She continued, 'When you walk a spiritual life, you won't be compatible with most souls. You feel more alone. Try not to look at what's happening to you as a form of punishment. You're being tested. You've chosen to walk a spiritual path.'

GWEN

Six months later Gwen opened with, 'It feels like you're banging your head against a wall.' This was accurate. I was now in year four of applying for a permanent job, because I thought it was my moral duty to do so. She gave me the initial M, which stood for Maeve, my maternal grandmother's name.

'What's needed now,' she continued, 'is the realisation that we can't always force our will upon something you think you need, or you think is for you. If something isn't happening for you, maybe it's not for you.'

Absolute gold!

Then, 'Who has diabetes?' My dad had recently been diagnosed with Type 2 Diabetes, but my sense is that this comment was about what was coming Sonny's way.

Again, readings can veer from one topic to another.

'It's about allowing what your gut instinct is telling you,' Gwen continued. 'They're telling you to go with what feels right, and the money will come to you. Trust is the only way forward; you need to believe they have your back.

'You've been through the hardest bit and cleared a lot of Karma, you've been clearing out old ways of thinking.

'Have you been taking photographs?' Gwen continued. 'Taking photographs will not only feed your soul but your tummy too.' On maternity leave I'd taught myself how to use a digital camera and within two years had turned professional.

'All they're trying to do is keep you on your plan,' she added. 'It feels imperative that we need to do something to bring in the bacon, but once you relax and trust and ride the wave, things will flow.

'They're showing you on a boat and the tide's coming in but you're rowing the wrong way. You think something, but your higher self knows differently.

'Why are they showing me rubbing an elbow?' This confirmation was dropped in randomly. I'd been suffering from elbow pain for a few weeks.

'They're showing me, they're with you and telling you to trust them,' Gwen said. 'It's something you've had to go through, it's all part of your plan – you wouldn't be willing to try something else otherwise.

'Who loves dancing? Dancing does for your mum what taking photographs do for you. Her mum keeps watching over her. She's proud of her and she's proud of you because of your creative artistic sides.

'I know you think you haven't achieved much, but you have. You can make a difference just by being you.'

Then Gwen made reference to that brief soulmate I had.

'You feel let down?' she asked. 'He was put there for a reason, to show you that there is life again. He came in to let you know that you won't be on your own forever.

'The person you're destined to be with is definitely out there,' she said. 'You have a few more steps to go through before he'll come in. You can't miss him. I don't think he'll be that far away. It's destiny. You both need to be your best selves. When you hit that point, you can't help but meet him. He will be at a point in his life where he also wants someone who can match where he is in his journey, and then you can do that journey together.'

She added, 'When it's time for something to end, the universe will make you so uncomfortable for you to stay. That's when something else will sneak in. Life is like a filing cabinet – you can't open another drawer until the others are closed.'

MAGGIE

'You haven't got what you wanted in terms of social interaction,' she began, picking up on the anguish a year or so of online dating had brought me. 'You've made a lot of effort. You've gone on a few dates but they've not gone anywhere.

'One of the men you met was a total geek. He looks nice on the outside, but there's not much there. He couldn't wipe his bum without his mum there. You'd feel like you were banging your head against a wall with him. He'd be a disappointment. Compared to what he looks like. He's not in a position in his life to sustain a relationship.'

She was talking about someone I'd nicknamed him Gabriel because, I figured, with his 6'2" muscular physique and long wavy fair hair, he looked like the Angel Gabriel, minus the wings. She'd really picked up on how disappointed I was when I didn't hear from him again after we'd got on so well.

'There'll be new people coming into your life by the 5th of January,' she continued. 'In January your business will really begin to take off. And meeting new people means a new energy around you. You're going to meet someone who's a precursor to your future man.

'Don't worry about age because you're young at heart. Someone will come in for you at the end of February and you'll go on a date.'

None of this came to pass.

GWEN

There was a pattern with these readings. Amazingly accurate descriptions and inspiring guidance, interspersed with inaccurate predictions!

'Your separation was a freeing experience,' Gwen began, referring to my separation with Sam just over two years prior. 'You've got to stop overthinking things. There's a plan for everyone, and everything is coming together in your plan. It might not feel like it. Why don't you look at your interests? They can make you money. But you've got to follow your interests because of the joy they bring, not just for the money they may make you.

'As far as your mental health is concerned, it's better for you to be without a job than get to the end of the week doing a job you don't like,' she added. 'We have to enjoy what we do. It's better to be short of money but be able to smile.

'The universe has been making the most of the coronavirus pandemic. As we've gone back into our homes, it's given us the time to rethink things. We've all got to reassess and rethink things. The whole world is going to change in much better ways as a result.

'The separation knocked your confidence. There's something out there waiting for you, I know there is. In the next nine months buying a house will be well within your grasp. You'll also be in a position to buy yourself a new car.' Neither of these predictions came true.

'There might be a course you want to do,' she continued. This bit did come true, I embarked on an adult learning course a few months later.

'Use your intuition more. You don't use it enough.' This was also true; I'd fallen into a state of despondency and been speaking to Quentin far less.

'You're working towards your destiny,' she offered next. 'There was a karmic connection with Sam, that's what kept you together for so long. But it ran its course.'

She predicted a new soulmate within twelve months.

'You've made some changes to how you think. This has meant it's possible for that person to come in. You can put that on the back burner knowing he'll be there. You're not meant to go through life without him. When the time's right, and as soon as he's ready, he'll come in.

'March and April – they're going to be very good months,' she continued. 'Put yourself out there. Make a business plan, send your CV around.' It was still the height of the Pandemic and the country was in lockdown. My contract with the local authority ended in late July and I found myself without work of any kind.

Nevertheless, Gwen said, 'I have no doubt whatsoever that you'll be fine where work is concerned.' This was true, during my freelance life I was never out of work, and I set up my own business later that year.

I asked why I hadn't got any of the dozens of jobs I'd applied for, and then my maternal grandmother came through to tell me they 'wouldn't have been right' for me. Gwen started up again about the man who was due to come my way. 'He dresses nicely and is very self-aware,' she offered. 'You are definitely going to meet him. He's going to be easy on the eye. And chivalrous. You need to find your inner calm,' she advised. 'That's when you'll meet someone who lives by that.'

And she said, as she had done before, that Sonny was a star child. 'They're amazing,' she added. 'They're full of light.'

'Good things can't happen to you if you feel like you don't deserve them,' she concluded.

MAGGIE

The Pandemic now behind us, I spoke to Maggie a few months later.

'Your grandad on your dad's side is here. He's been gone a long time. He's showing me pictures of you with him aged between eight and twelve years old.' This made me chuckle because my grandad had always been a staunch atheist.

'The split from your husband was the right thing for both of you. I want you to ask many more questions before you date someone. No one's separated enough at the school gate,' she continued, 'you don't want to leave your town, you'll stay in that house until you meet someone.' I didn't. Our landlords sold the house twelve months later and Sonny and me had to move, but, again, things change.

'It'll be three years until you move in with someone and your two families will be brought together.' This precise prediction always worried me, given that there is no sense of time on the Other Side, and what with all the other variable factors.

'Change your upper age limit on the dating apps,' she continued. 'He'll be in his early fifties, very good looking, like George Clooney, in a suit, shirt and tie which is slightly off centre, a university professor of something like astrophysics. But he'll be cute and scatterbrained.

'What I love about him is the talking. You'll build an amazing platform for your relationship, talking and philosophising into the night. Don't worry if he's not romantic, he won't look at anyone else.

'Your first date will be a physical one. You'll go cycling together. But the way you like to cycle is different; you go mountain biking for aerobic exercise, like an athlete, while he likes long-distance road cycling. It'll be very soon. August.'

August came and went. The positive that can be taken from the plethora of men that were predicted to come along for me over the course of these five years, but never did, is that there is more than one suitor out there for us.

'You're borderline hyperactive. You need the physical element to offset the mental energy.'

TAMSIN

Six months later, I spoke to Tamsin again.

'September is a very significant month for you,' she said. 'Like, you'll come out of a shell having partially changed your outlook regarding the next stage of your life.

'Aspects of your personality have been dying off, and new understandings have started to grow, and aspects of your old self are in the throes of dying off because they no longer serve you.

'I can feel a sense of *hang on in there* with you.

'New people are going to come in to present opportunities for you so you can come out of this reflective time and springboard into a new way. And that involves your work.

'You'll meet someone completely new, but he'll slip under your radar,' she continued. 'You won't even consider him, you'll dance around each other before you realise he's someone significant.

'I'm getting you travelling to London, on top of working from home,' she continued. 'At some point from September to Christmas there'll definitely be a change with your job, a new boss.'

'Go with the flow this year,' she finished. 'Nothing you push for will happen. Just relax and be hands off for a bit, because even if you do try, it will be blocked.'

Another six months passed with none of the foreseen changes having come to fruition, so I spoke to Tamsin again for some more insight. This was to be my last reading, from then on preferring to trust my own intuition and guides.

'You're a very traditional family woman and family values are really important to you. When you love, you love in an unconditional way. You have the hand of Source on you because there's something going on around you causing you upset.

'You're clearly a spiritual lady. Your guide has stepped in close to help you make decisions.

'You have a lot of spiritual support around you. It's a testing time for you at the moment. There's a sense of rumination, confusion and overthinking.

'You're all about balance and justice and people being fair and when those things are lacking it upsets you. In October some kind of injustice is going to come back around and reveal itself in a more positive way.

'Your life is beset by confusion and feeling misunderstood.

'Your life purpose is to develop.

'There are many paths that lead to Source.

'Mother Nature is extremely important to you.

'Your third eye was open when you were born. You chose to be a mother and a partner, and you chose a spiritual life.

'You have been sent a test of resilience. There is always a way forward. You'll always get over those hurdles. The journey is more important than the finish line.'

Then she talked about my past.

'What has happened to you isn't very nice. There was a confrontation. There was an aspect of control there. When you tried reasoning with him, he became defensive quite quickly.' I couldn't believe that the Other Side were still bringing up that horrible bloke from over two years ago!

'It is planned for you to settle back down in this lifetime,' she continued. 'In order for that to happen, you need to be visible, be out, be sociable. He'll be introduced to you by someone else at an event. He's self-employed and can work anywhere. It'll be this year or next year. He doesn't live close. You'll be going backwards and forwards to visit each other. He'll be younger than you. He's many fields away, maybe a county away. He doesn't put a lot of onus on money. Family values are extremely important to him. It will get going quite quickly. He's a massive animal lover and keeps bees.'

She continued, 'Your ex-partner is a doting dad. He has a lovely energy. He's an easy-going guy. He'll get on with your new partner.'

She gave me the letters F and S.

'You've got some lovely stuff coming in this year,' she said. 'I need to describe someone to you. He reminds me of the actor who was in *'The Theory of Everything'* (Eddie Redmayne, I found out via Google later). He's a man of the land, loves horticulture and agriculture and loves being outside. He's happy in jeans and jumper. He had a woolly jumper on in my meditation.

'He is the catalyst which is going to change what you're doing. Do you work with vulnerable people?' I explained that I did indirectly because one of my clients worked with vulnerable people and I worked pro bono for a number of charities. 'You're going to be more directly involved,' she continued.

'It's going to be a busy couple of years coming up. Don't think you're not good enough. You've got to stop that self-doubt; it's not serving you. They know you love animals and the outdoors and you're going to own a house with land, and that's going to come through him.

'There's another direction that you're meant to be going in. Some of your animals will be used to bring out a positive future for disadvantaged young people who will come to your land.

'I can see you living high up on the clifftops. You'll move into this large apartment, which is part of a large old house with phenomenal views.

'He's quiet, thoughtful, muscular and strong. You'll meet him anytime this year. I think through friends, in a social setting, though he'll be the quiet one in the group.

'The universe is bringing him to you. He's lovely. Mid-thirties. I definitely saw sheep and goats. I'm pretty sure he decides to be a sheep farmer. And you'll have one or two horses. He was leaning on a spade when I saw him.

'Sonny will go to college and learn about horticulture and agriculture. He's always going to be sports-orientated.

'It's set in stone.

'This man has been unlucky with losing people to illness, but he's inherited money. You won't have a massive mortgage. I can see you purchasing a property together. I feel quite sad for him in a lot of ways. He hasn't got any children and doesn't have a big family. But he's not concerned about it.

'Sonny will really bond with him. He'll have a simple name like Steve or Simon. But he's a complex character. Scruffy, fair skinned, ruddy. Brown hair. Gentle. Thoughtful. Not a big drinker.

'Reach out to spirit in lonely times and ask them to fill that void with their unconditional love.'

I never did meet my Eddie Redmayne.

Quentin told me that he didn't see the same future as she did, and, 'She gets carried away sometimes.'

Although I'd appreciated other mediums' insights, which confirmed what I already 'knew', I was fatigued with their prophesies never coming to pass. I never doubted that they weren't extraordinary mediums, and that they were simply passing on what their guides were telling them, using all the available information at the time, and I knew never to live by the predictions of a medium or psychic, but it seemed pointless now. As things calmed down in my life emotionally, and clarity returned, it was my own intuition and my own guide to whom I'd listen, I reconciled.

CHAPTER 17
BELLE

WE SET UP OUR OWN shelter, a large, robust three-room tent on the edge of the river. And so began our last few weeks on Earth. Over the coming days, as well as Florence and her family and Sam, we were joined by more individuals, couples and families from across Canada. We learnt that at least one member of each group had received the same message from their guide, instructing them to head to Peace River, before a visit from Black Claw.

Our guides also told us that there were numerous rendezvous points across the globe. Safe pockets where those who listened would be rescued. During their lives, most of the psychics in our now sixty-person camp had received some sort of intelligence that there were other life forms out there. But while we couldn't help but laugh at the incredulous prospect that we were going to come face-to-face with alien life and be whisked off on a UFO to another planet, all of us were overwhelmed with the dreadful prospect of the destruction of the planet and the end of life on Earth as we knew it.

Our days were spent fishing on the lake, swimming in the lake, exercising and enjoying the warm summer sun, nature's playground. Here, consumerism and materialism had no meaning, and here, we were all equal, no matter what our educational backgrounds or former social standing.

Among us were the doctors from Saskatoon and their teenage boys; the vegan punk rock singer from Vancouver, his seamstress girlfriend and her eight-year-old daughter; cattle farmers from Red Deer; a pharmacologist, his HR-manager wife and their son and daughter, from Victoria; and several First Nations families. The diversity in our community made for fascinating stories around the fire. Our bond was our spirituality. I'd always felt like spiritualism was like a secret club. More than ever, it felt a privilege to be a part of it.

We would tell each other our stories. One of us was Belle, who had made the journey from Calgary with her husband Aaron and their six children. This is what she told us...

I was very much in tune with spirit right from the beginning of my life on Earth. I remember being a baby and angels visiting me. One gave me a message about my life purpose, he said, 'You're here to help humanity.' They used to visit every now and again and sit on the end of my bed and talk to me when I was tiny.

I saw them, and other spirits, with my physical eyes, but as I grew older they took a step back and faded, although I always knew they were with me.

I was seven years old when my maternal grandad died. That night he came and sat on the end of my bed too as I was drifting off to sleep. At first I was a bit unsettled, especially because he didn't say anything but just smiled and brushed his hair before disappearing.

He had brought me my first piano when I was three years old. Once he passed on, I would always smell his old pipe smoke enter the room when I was practicing and feel him sat behind me enjoying my practice. When I started my musical grading, he would always come with me to the exams too. He loved that I played music, and I'm sure he had a part in opening so many musical opportunities for me as I grew older.

Dreamtime was my favourite. I would spend my nighttime traveling the astral plane, time travelling and tuning into animals. I felt so much freedom and so much at ease being with spirit, which was very different from my waking time.

My mum and dad were especially afraid about the thought of seeing spirits so they didn't want to hear about it. The only person I had to talk to about it was my paternal grandad. His dad had been a keen spiritualist and was desperate to make contact with the Other Side, but never did.

My grandad on the other hand was sure something was there and had many experiences with spirit but maintained he was never psychic or had a gift. It helped having someone to talk to and listen to me, without ever laughing or saying, 'You're crazy,' or trying to explain it away with logic.

I spent a lot of time with Grandad growing up. We used to practice telepathy, although I didn't know it at the time. I thought it was just a fun guessing game. We'd sit for ages doing it, and gradually the guessing turned into knowing. I could clearly receive his messages through my mind.

By the time I reached high school, I'd realised not everyone saw the world the same way I did, so it was a part of me I hid away. I found it hard in friendships, feeling completely misunderstood – and a bit weird! Was I the only one who knew about the Other Side?

I saw it made people uncomfortable. I remember being really confused. People walking around, living their lives like this is all there is. They suffer, live in pain, and are afraid of dying, when there is a whole other world of support and love that wants to help them. If they had seen what I saw, they would never be afraid of dying.

I didn't know how to deal with the pain and confusion of this. People – the world, I guess – living so far away from their soul and spiritual nature.

I had two people close to me who died very quickly during this period, although they came straight through to me to say goodbye, I was mad. Mad that they had left me, and that they got to go 'home'. Mad that I was here and had to wait until I was much older to be able to do what I was here to do. Was I just supposed to wait for everyone else to catch up?

I shut it all out. No more spirit. I doubted if any of these experiences were even real, questioning everything. I didn't even want to believe I was here to help anymore.

Music continued to be my medicine and solace. At sixteen, I left home and went to music college to study classical music full time.

At first I really felt like for the first time I was happy and living life, but in the years that followed I became really depressed and by the time I turned nineteen, I developed a serious form of cluster headaches which rendered me unable to work and play music. I felt locked in my mind and unable to move my body.

A year later I became pregnant with my first daughter by my boyfriend at the time. Everyone was worried about how I would manage and cope, being so poorly, but there was something within me that knew this was perfect. The shift in hormones actually helped me manage my pain better and I began to feel better than I'd felt in a long time.

When my daughter was finally here and we got home, I remember crying while holding her. It was the first time in a long time I had felt full soul memory activation. I had a reason to keep going, and being a mother was so natural to me. I intuitively knew how to do it, the wisdom of past lives and even past lives spent with my daughter came back. She literally saved me from taking my own life. She gave me a reason to live again. I felt like my intuition was back. It was different and didn't work like it did before, but it was there.

Soon after her birth we moved into a house behind a graveyard and very soon I started seeing spirits with my physical eye walking through the front door, through the house and out the back door. I'd see their shadows outside the bay window and then there would be a rush of air as the front door swung open as they entered the house.

One night I was visited by two ladies called Anna and Sue. They were local spirits who used to pass through the row of terraced house we lived in, as they walked an old public pathway. Anna told me that they'd come to help me look after my daughter who was really ill as a baby.

Part of her condition involved her being sick in the night which would result in her stopping breathing. Every time she was about to be sick, they'd communicate with me in my sleep and wake me up. And every time I would get to her just as she woke and was sick.

As my daughter got older I could see her communicating with them too. Waves, smiles and even kisses goodbye. I am so grateful to Anna and Sue for helping us.

I eventually split up with my daughter's dad and met another man. He was really psychic and we bonded over this. He was the first person I spoke to that understood all my experiences and could actually help me tune into it more. But he was also an alcoholic, and he would beat me up when he was drunk.

One time he strangled me and I almost died. I grabbed my daughter and his son, who were sleeping in other rooms, and ran to a neighbour's house and he came and started throwing bricks at the window. He'd keep apologising and I'd always take him back.

This was the first time I could understand the separation between our soul and our human selves. The thing that made me stay was his soul, the reason I should have left was his human. I think I thought I could save him, but looking back, I can see I was also so afraid of losing the connection I had to spirit, with him.

To add to the confusion, I went to see a psychic and she told me, 'You're meant to be together'. That afternoon when I got home, my grass woven outdoor mat started smoking. I threw water on it and kept turning it round to try and stop it from burning. But it just kept reigniting and burning. It burnt for about three hours. When I went back out to check on it later, a perfect cross had been burnt in the middle of the mat. I got a strong sense that I was safe and I was protected. And that the psychic had been wrong.

That night when I was asleep, I was given a message that in two days' time he was going to beat me up again and then they showed me what was going to happen. They told me that this would be the end of it, and not to panic.

Two days later, on Saturday night, I was sat watching TV and he started kicking off at me, just as I'd been told that he would. So I took the kids, left the house, and went. It was just as they had shown me, and our relationship ended right there and then.

I found out much later, during a past life regression session with another psychic, that his behaviour was due to past life stuff. He'd been a warlock and I'd been a witch, and he'd strangled me in that life too.

I moved house after that and ended up in another relationship and having my second child. Anna and Sue didn't come with us. I was really upset about that!

The house I moved into was owned by a lovely family. But the house was meant for their son, who had recently died suddenly in his twenties from a heart attack. They were so sad about his death. Within a week of moving in he kept coming through to me saying, 'You have to tell them I'm sorry, I didn't mean to leave them so suddenly, I didn't know I was going.' I would wake in the night in floods of tears feeling his sadness.

Being able to pass on these his messages to his family showed me how much peace I could bring to people who are grieving.

I became close with the family, especially his younger brother. When he visited me, his older brother in spirit would usually come too. He'd walk in with him and join in the conversation with us!

I could feel spirit desperate for me to fully open back up again, but I was still reluctant. I had enrolled on a course to become a complementary therapist at the local college. I thought maybe massage and reflexology would be the route to helping people. During the first session of reflexology we were invited to place our hands on the other person's feet to do some simple grounding exercises. I placed my hands on my partner and breathed deeply. Another soul memory activation came through. My partner immediately burst into tears as her body just unlocked all the tension and stress. I realised as I looked at her feet, that I could read them like a story book.

It was all there, her emotions, her personality, her past and her future. I couldn't believe it. I had heard of palm reading but never heard of foot reading. I qualified as a therapist and quickly became known as the foot whisperer in the area.

I was cautious, and unconfident at this point. Spirit started working with me in a new way; it felt like files of information were just getting dropped in my head. I called it 'drop box'; I didn't know how I knew things, but I just had to trust it. No signs, no sights, no hearing, I just had to say what was in my mind. It was hard, and I held back a lot. I didn't want to hurt anyone, or scare anyone off for that matter.

As luck would have it, the lady who I signed up to receive a Reiki attunement with was also a psychic medium. She took me under her wing for a bit and this really accelerated my senses again.

During the Reiki attunement, I asked spirit to show me the truth. I can laugh now, but the answer was tough. I laugh because I naively thought 'show me the truth' would be like spirit lifting the stage curtain and hearing a massive 'ta-dah'. It was anything but. Within five days, I found out my partner was being unfaithful, had hidden tens of thousands of pounds from me, and was partaking in some other dodgy dealings.

This was the truth I had asked to see.

I knew I had to leave.

It was this window of opportunity that saw me move back to Calgary.

Another fresh slate and new beginning.

Those ten years were rough. Although painful, opening myself back to spirit somehow felt like I had found myself again. Everything up to that point was hard, painful and challenging, and I'm sure that's because I had shut it all down. I wasn't particularly willing to accept help or be guided. Protected, yes, I never said no to that, but I came to see that every time they stepped in to help was because I had pushed it to the absolute edge and things were about to go really wrong.

I know now that opening myself back up was actually coming 'home' and remembering my true self. Moving forward I wanted to work with spirit to help me expand and make life better, not just to get me through the dark times.

I had no idea how I was going to get to back to Calgary and had little to no money.

I started automatic writing again and asked about moving back. My maternal grandad came straight through and told me I was going to get an apartment on a certain road in a certain suburb, and I was going to get a job at a spa, both before August.

I visited a few weeks later for a job interview at a spa and to view an apartment. Grandad was with me as I went to the interview, so I knew I was in the right place. When I went to visit the apartment, I felt him around me again, but the place was in a terrible state. It had been trashed by the previous tenant. The agent upon opening the door said, 'You are the only person we've had to see this apartment, I hope you've got some vision.'

There was faeces in the corner of the room, blood up the walls, and fist marks through the internal walls. I was having second thoughts, but Grandad was insistent; this was the apartment. So I followed him and put in the application. Six weeks later I'd moved in and got the job. Luckily the apartment was completely refurbished. Apart from needing to cleanse and clear the energy in there, it was perfect. This was my first taste of flow and alignment with spirit. I couldn't believe how easy it all came together.

I was starting to hear spirit clearly again now and at this point, while I'd hidden it in the past, I didn't have a filter when it came to being open about it. Trying to make a good impression on my new boss, when I was chatting to her one day, I passed on a message that her grandad was coming through really strongly for her. She suddenly burst into tears and said, 'He died yesterday.'

She was a few weeks pregnant and he'd told me she was going to lose her baby, but she would have another. Two weeks later she did lose her unborn child. He wanted me to help, so I did some fertility reflexology with her. A few weeks later she became pregnant again and went on to have a healthy baby.

Another colleague at the spa was getting married at the weekend. I had my Tarot cards in my bag and during our lunch break she asked me to read for her. Happily, I shuffled and pulled three cards. There was a very clear message on the cards that her marriage wouldn't last, and her future husband wasn't the love that she wanted or needed.

I broke into a sweat, not knowing how I could ever pass on a message like that, two days before her wedding. I knew she knew that I was holding back. I didn't tell her.

Two years later, I met her again. She'd come to see me at my business space. She told me, 'We aren't together anymore, but you already knew that didn't you?' She wasn't angry with me, and we talked it through. She said that if she had been in the same position as me, she would have done the same thing, and she said she still would have married him even if I had told her, because she didn't see a way out of the relationship at that time. Deep down she knew it too, she admitted, the cards were just a confirmation. Hearing her say this relieved a lot of guilt and pressure I had felt holding the message back.

Six weeks after starting the job at the spa, I got a message from the boss to come into work the next day for a meeting. I got a message from spirit saying, 'Take your uniform in with you'. I walked into the meeting and put my uniform on the desk. And they said, 'How did you know?' I was like, 'Come off it!' They just said I hadn't passed my probation. At the time I thought it was probably because I had freaked them out, and their clients too!

A few days later, spirit told me to go into this particular nail salon saying, 'Ask about the room in the back'. I literally had about $20 in the bank at this point, but my guides told me I didn't have to worry.

The shop owner said yes straightaway and I started my own business from the treatment room there. I had only been back in town for seven weeks, I had no website, no social media or business-related material. Just me and my hands. Again, spirit said not to worry and leave it to them. From that day on I've never looked back.

Shortly after Christmas in 2016, my guides told me I needed to go internet dating. I ignored that message for a while. But then every day someone at work would suddenly say, as if out of nowhere, 'You need to go on internet dating', and then go back to what they were saying. So I knew this was spirit's way of getting the message across to me.

By the end of the week, I gave in and set up a profile on a dating site. Within an hour I had a message from someone, saying, 'Do you think we could talk on the phone?' We spoke for three hours solid. Aaron was a healer and intuitive too. It felt like light bulbs were going off in my body. Spirit poured in the room. The next morning I lay in bed thinking about our conversation the night before. Excited but also wary. I didn't want to be hurt again.

Next, I hear, 'You can come off the dating site now.'

Our relationship developed quickly and deeply, but also enhanced our own individual senses and energy. We went into business together, got married, blended our families together and had two more children together.

I couldn't believe how my life was opening up. A beautiful family, a thriving business doing what I loved, a loving relationship, and my health was improving by the day. My confidence in being true to myself, true to my spirit, was transforming my life.

For all the times in my life where I begged spirit to take me back because it was so hard to be here, for the times I wanted to give up and fantasised about ending it all, to know they were with me and that they loved me unconditionally, I am so, so grateful. I can't imagine ever moving through all that without them. I am so grateful I waited for better days.

It was 2018, and I'd just had my first baby with Aaron when I developed sepsis. As I lay in my hospital bed and felt myself rise above my body looking down on myself, I could feel and hear spirit all around me in the room. It was like a meeting. They said to me, 'What do you want to do?' Flashes of my life, the lessons and the experiences were all being collected in a library.

I had the choice whether to stay on Earth, or return to spirit. I looked at my daughter and just thought, 'My life is just beginning, I'm going to stay'. And then it felt like I was jolted back, like a sheet had been whipped off the top of me, like a layer of me was taken away.

I started to fight the infection and get better from that moment. A host of angels stayed in my private room for the duration of my stay in hospital. I knew things had to change in terms of my physical health. From that point on I never asked to go back again.

By this point my relationship and experience with spirit had become a lot more integrated in my day-to-day life. Walking with spirit is just how I live my life. It feels like a flow, with less of the big neon signs saying, 'This is a message!' It's a steady, constant, loving presence that's always there just guiding me through.

I have witnessed profound and miraculous healings in treatment. Angels singing over lost souls, grandparents and ancestors passing babies to women who couldn't get pregnant. Babies communicating their chosen names to their parents. Beautiful reunions between spirit and the living, bringing much peace to the grief-stricken heart. Spontaneous healing and psychic surgery of the body given from spirit. Even babies being turned in the uterus by archangels.

I had a friend who had been in labour for a long time and kept in regular contact with me throughout, while it wasn't progressing. The doctors had threatened an intervention, which she really didn't want to have. I remember being on the school run when I received her message. I immediately sat on a grassy area with the kids and asked them to play while I tuned in for her.

Her baby was stuck somewhere in the birth canal which was why he wasn't traveling down. I knew she didn't have long before they intervened as both baby and mum were so tired, so I called on Archangel Gabriel who oversees babies being born.

As I sat in quiet meditation I watched Archangel Gabriel turn her baby and saw him drop down further into the birth canal.

That was all that was needed. I went home to wait for an update. An hour later, I received a message to say he was finally here, and well. No intervention needed.

My own experience wasn't so dissimilar when I had my last baby in 2020. He too was stuck into my hip, and although my labour was progressing quickly and no intervention was threatened, both my husband and I knew our baby boy needed a little assistance.

Aaron held his hand just above my hip where he was stuck and we both felt a massive surge of energy move between us. It was like a magnetic force guided his head out of place. Just like when I had sepsis and felt angelic intervention, the room when quiet and time stood still. Within five minutes, he arrived.

In my early forties, I had one of the most profound experiences I've ever had, helping my paternal grandad and my beloved friend pass over. Both happened in a short space of time.

It felt like an initiation into a deeper understanding of how life works and why we are here. I had spent a lot of time working with birth and conception, and now I was to understand death and dying.

Four months prior to my grandad having a heart attack, I was woken in the night by his wife, my grandma (who was already in spirit). She told me he was dying and would be leaving the earth plane soon. I told my parents to prepare and make the most of their time together, but they didn't believe me. He was well in himself and they held on to what a gypsy had told them years before, that he was going to live into his nineties.

But in the early hours, one Saturday morning, my grandad had a heart attack and my (much older) friend had a fall. In the hours leading up to going to bed the night before, I felt I was being prepared for something, but there was no particular message.

Both my grandad and my friend were taken into hospital that weekend. In the first instance, the hospital said Grandad would be fine and was being kept in for general observations, likely to be discharged the next day. Sunday morning came, and my husband and I decided to change our plans. We didn't quite know why, but just that the day needed to be kept open.

Aaron, due to drop his children home later that evening, decided to pop into hospital on his way past to see my grandad. I took the rest of the children on a walk. While I was out walking, my uncle in spirit told me Grandad had internal bleeding and would die soon. I had no signal on my phone but could feel Aaron psychically connecting with me wanting to talk.

As soon as I got signal my phone started to ring. It was Aaron. He said, 'I need you to stop and breathe a moment.' I said, 'It's OK, Uncle Joe has told me.' The doctors had given him two hours to live because of the internal bleeding. I went to the hospital with my parents and left Aaron with the children.

He relaxed as soon as I got there. 'I'm glad you're here,' he said to me. 'I've had a good innings, I've had the best time.' I said, 'It's all right now, I'll see you across. Everybody is here waiting for you.' He smiled. I sat and meditated with him. He could see everyone around him in spirit and he was waving at them! He was ready, but his body wasn't, quite yet. It was ironic as the person who had taught me so much as a kid was still teaching me even as he died.

He made it through the night and I went and sat with him in the morning so my parents could get some sleep. I held his hand and journeyed with him. I was shown how the body has to lighten and resolve before it can leave. It was like his body was telling a story in fast forward mode. Energy clearing, emotions being processed, life lessons coming together. I saw the same library I visited when I had sepsis. Eventually things settled down. His soul was moving in and out of his body, but his etheric cord to the Earth was winding up.

As the hours passed, his soul spent more time out of his body, and he was talking to spirit. He was joined by old friends and family, and of course his wife who he missed greatly.

He was at last ready to leave. Upon sunrise as the soft orange glow crept into his room, he took his last breath.

I wasn't with him at that point. I was at home, and woke up as he took his last breath. A familiar knowing I had experienced throughout my life. It feels like the gunshot from *The Hunger Games* film, when a Tribute dies. It rippled through my body.

I made Grandad promise to visit me. Sure enough, within a few hours I felt him come to me. I was overwhelmed with grief and love. He stepped into my body and said, 'This is how good I feel, I'm so light, and so free.'

He's with me and around my kids so much. He was known as 'cheeky grandad', and I can tell you, he's just as cheeky in spirit as he was on Earth. I often catch him laughing with the kids and playing with my parents' dog. He sits at the dinner table when we gather for Sunday roast all together and is quick to give the kids a hug when they need one. They love him so much. We all do.

It has been a hard thing to marry the sadness I felt losing Grandad and having a completely different relationship with him in spirit.

I also still had a soul contract with my friend to oversee her passing.

My dear friend Gloria was one-hundred-and-one when her spine collapsed. She lost her independence overnight. It was hard seeing someone's body give up before her mind and spirit were ready. She wanted to die, but it was a long process for her. From the summer onwards, she was in and out of consciousness. Just like I had seen with Grandad, her soul moved in and out of her body.

She spent days at a time with spirit. I visited her every day, sometimes we would talk and other times I would just sit with her while she spoke. Everyone said she was slowly dying and it could be months before she passed. Her body was strong, and she continued to eat and drink when she felt like it. One night, a few hours after I'd left her, chatty and spoon feeding her fish pie, spirit asked me to do some healing with her.

I could see her divine spark. Not just hers; spirit showed me everybody's divine spark, just gently dancing around a few feet above our heads where our soul star chakra is. It's the essence of the divine that resides in our being. Our connection to God, and all that is. It's different to our soul, more like life force energy. It's the creative energy or the battery source for our human experience. During the healing I felt her soul-heart energy and her etheric cord spiral up back to her divine spark. Her soul had left her body and I knew it wouldn't be going back.

The following day, she didn't wake at all. The nurses said she was just tired and sleepy. I knew it was only a matter of time. That night I woke many times in the night. At 6am the nurse phoned to say there was a change and asked me if I wanted to come in.

I arrived with her soon afterwards and just like with Grandad, meditated and journeyed with her. After forty-five minutes I felt my awareness come back into the room, like spirit was drawing my presence upon her in the physical. In my mind's eye, I saw that she was being showered with magnolia petals; magnolia is the flower of unconditional love.

I was watching all these flowers fall down on her. The room was peaceful and serene, another moment where time stood still. I held her hand and I said the Lord's Prayer, which was really important to her. As I got to the end of the prayer, she took her last breath.

It was incredibly surreal. I suddenly felt all the tiredness and grief of the last six months come crashing down into my body.

In a daze, later that morning, sat in bed looking out of the window, I saw a flock of birds flying together in perfect unison outside. They came so close to my bedroom window. And I just heard, 'We're all one. Like in birth, like in breathing, like in death'.

Life and death come from exactly the same place. How we come in is how we go out. This is how the universe works. You are made of the very thing that connects you to everything.

CHAPTER 18
NEW LIFE NEXT PARTY

THERE WAS NO WARNING. We woke to the news on the radio one morning that Western nations had been served an ultimatum; to withdraw their presence from anywhere other than within their own borders, or face 'consequences'. If Western governments didn't heed this autocrat's warning, in seven days, no city in the Western world would be safe, his team asserted.

We listened to the news with stunned silence. The next few days came and went with no reconciliation. The airwaves were rife with politicians, political scientists and ordinary citizens of the West and East debating both academic and emotional stances.

Then everything went dead. Our efforts to find ways to link with the world outside our secret commune on Rainbow Lake went unrewarded as we knew, individually, and collectively, that the death of the world as we knew it, at the hands of mankind, was underway.

Two days later the inconceivable happened. As dusk fell, a soft far-off hum became a throbbing whirring noise which began to vibrate the ground we stood on, as a yellow, pink and orange glow crept over the hills until the lake became an iridescent white. The glow turned into a glaring light, too bright to look at.

A giant black and silver spherical aircraft descended over the lake, hovering above us and sending a vibration over the water, which was so strong giant ripples covered its surface manifesting as small waves by our feet. We stood on the shoreline, motionless, arms around each other, staring at this thing above us, waiting for the door to open.

As we waited, and stared, and held one another, I comprehended at last, the truth. Not just my truth, or our truth, but the universe's truth. I turned to Sonny, and the others, and told them, 'I know why we're here. It's just to love each other. We're all one big family, really.'

FRIENDS' EXPERIENCES

AMY

My first experience with the spirit world happened at my dad's house in the hamlet of Altarnun on Bodmin Moor, Cornwall. It was a three-bedroom semi-detached cottage with parts of it dating back to the 15th century. As a child when I visited him it always felt creepy; I used to feel scared about being in my room and in the hallway but I used to wonder if this was just because it was an old house. As I grew older I had the sense of being watched and felt even more uneasy in my own room.

Then when I was in my teens, poltergeist activity started up. I heard a door slam downstairs, when there was no draught. I saw an apparition of a woman downstairs, which appeared to dissolve right in front of me. And one evening while I was lying in bed, I felt cold hands moving up my legs. My dad called the local vicar over. The vicar said he found a really angry man located at the top of the stairs right next to my room, who was stuck there and needed guiding into the light. There was never anything else after that.

A few years later, while I was living at a friend's house near Boscastle, north Cornwall, I had more experiences. I stayed there for around eight months in total. It was another old house located down a quiet lane. Within a few months, things started happening. One afternoon, I came in and was downstairs in the kitchen drinking a coffee by the AGA and heard the loudest bang on the floor upstairs. I thought, what on earth is that, and went upstairs thinking it must have been the cat knocking something over. But the cat was curled up asleep on the bed. And there, on the floor, was a giant 10kg cannon ball, which was kept on the dressing table as an ornament. My hair stood on end.

I just thought it was really bizarre and that's when I thought, oh my god, I wonder if this place is haunted. I picked up the ball and put it back on the dresser.

A few weeks later I moved the bedroom furniture around, including my bed, situating it between two doors; one was my bedroom door into the hallway and the other, a locked door into the adjoining, next door house. That night, I woke up to the feeling like someone was walking over me. I told my boyfriend who was lying next to me and he said he'd felt it too. It was as though this was their usual walkway through the doors, and my bed was now blocking it.

Despite this, I didn't move my bed back. Then a few days later I came home and sat on my bed, it was around 6pm and dark outside and I had my friend's little Jack Russel with me. Then, all of a sudden, I felt my hair stand on end and the dog started yapping and running around the bed. Then, the bed started violently shaking. It lasted a few seconds. I jumped off the bed and ran out of the house with the dog. I was so freaked out. I got in my car and drove up the road to ring my friend, who said she'd come straight home.

She came back and I told her I thought maybe it was because they didn't like my bed blocking their walkway. That night I felt bed paralysis, like someone was strangling me. It was so vivid it was like it was actually happening, and yet you know you're asleep and you can't wake up. I've never had it before or since.

The next day my friend said, 'I think I should let you know that the woman who used to live here got killed in a car accident. A car crashed into the car she was in and her seatbelt cut her throat.'

I moved the bed back after that and nothing really happened from then on, but I left pretty soon afterwards because I hated living there after that.

When I lived in Looe, I rented a room in a house with my boyfriend – in the most haunted cottage in the town, apparently, although I found this out after I moved out. My landlady did tell me it was haunted, but the ghost, called Eliza, was lovely, she said.

I was supposed to meet my landlady, who was also my friend, in the pub one evening and was upstairs in my room getting ready when I thought I heard her come home. I heard what sounded like loads of bags being rustled in the kitchen. So I went down the stairs to look and the noise carried on until I got to the bottom step, when it abruptly stopped. There was nothing in the kitchen so I went to look in the living room and the footrests on the whole three-seater sofa were up. You have to forcibly pull a leaver to put the footrests up, which we only did if we were actually sitting on the sofa, and always put them back down when we got up. I just thought, 'Oh my god,' and ran out to the pub. My landlady just said that it was probably Eliza. My boyfriend also said he felt someone pushing past him on the stairs once.

A few months after we moved out, I went to visit my former landlady and as soon as I walked in, I heard footsteps walking across the hallway upstairs, directly above us. I asked her if someone was there and she said, 'No, it's Eliza.' I asked her if I could go and check because it sounded like someone really was walking around up there. Of course, there wasn't, and she just said, 'Told you!'

When I was living near Minions on Bodmin Moor, I also heard and felt a party blower being blown in my face, as loud as it is in real life. When I told my boyfriend, he said he didn't want to say anything, but it had happened to him too.

LINDA

In 1984, a gypsy came into the shop I was working in when I was sixteen and I gave her some vegetables to take away, and in return she told my fortune: she said, 'Tonight's the night you're going to meet the man that you'll marry.' That was the evening I met Gary. We went on to marry and we've been together ever since, around thirty years now.

Then, when my dad died in 1992, it wasn't long afterwards that our daughter Emily, who was only two at the time, started waving out the window at someone. We couldn't see anyone there so asked her who she was waving to and she said, 'Grampy', which is what she called my dad. She even described the T-shirt he had on, which was the one we put on him in his coffin. She said he was sat on the roof outside our kitchen window. Then the next day we went for a walk and all the clouds were racing across the sky and she looked up and said, 'Oh, look! Grampy's going back to Nanny's house.'

A few years later I went to see a medium at Arlington Court and she knew things that no one could have known. My brother had died four years before my dad, and she knew I had his leather coat and that I had a record of him singing. She told me she knew that I sensed a presence in my house and that the door opens sometimes and I always say hello. I did it because I felt my dad was always around.

She told me that a picture would fall off the wall the next time I felt that presence. I went home and told Gary what she had said and, just as I said the words, a massive map we had on the kitchen wall, peeled off and fell on the floor.

Emily and her friend, who were only young, screamed and jumped in my lap out of surprise, but I found it really comforting to know he was there.

HELENA

When I was seventeen, and living in Australia, I was so ill with food poisoning I ended up in hospital. It was a private hospital so no one was in the emergency room with me except for my mum.

The doctors asked me how much pain I was in, and at the time I said ten out of ten, so they got me some morphine in this big blue syringe. As soon as they gave me the morphine they asked me what my pain level was, so, again, I said ten out of ten because it hadn't started working yet. But within thirty seconds it kicked in, and before I could tell them it was working, they were already coming back with more, and I found myself unable to speak to stop them because the first dose had been so strong.

They gave me the second dose and I remember thinking, 'Whoa, this is pretty intense.' Then I decided to move my right index finger which was clamped in a pulse checker, and as I did so, I started to flatline. All these people rushed towards me putting oxygen on my face and doing other things to me, and I remember just wanting to tell them, 'I'm OK, I just moved my finger a little bit, I'm not flatlining.'

Then, I sat up, turned around and looked at the heart monitor and saw that it *was* flatlining. The beeping started up again and I went to sleep for a bit. In the middle of the night I woke up, and recalling what had happened, decided to wiggle my finger again. This time, nothing happened, the machine kept beeping as normal. So I wiggled it even more, and still, the machine kept beeping. I thought it was a bit weird and went back to sleep.

My mum came to pick me up the next morning and we started talking about what had happened and I said how crazy it was when I moved my finger and saw that I'd flatlined on the heart monitor, and how I sat up and saw them working on me. She looked at me and said, 'You never sat up, you were lying there with your eyes closed the whole time. It was really scary to see you like that.'

I realised I must have had an out of body experience where I left my body and was watching the doctors reviving me, while really, I was lying there with my eyes closed.

In 2014 when I was pregnant with my son, my aunt – who wasn't that much older than me, and who I was really close to – was killed in a small plane crash. I was really upset for a while and found myself really grappling over the fear she must have felt in the last moments, as the plane came down. About six months after her death, I had a dream in which she visited me. It was so powerful, it felt like she was really there in my room talking to me. I told her about my concerns for her and she told me that it wasn't actually that bad, and she was OK. I really do believe it was her coming to visit me to tell me this.

DAN

Growing up I wasn't a believer or a disbeliever. The first time I thought a spirit had helped me out was soon after I joined the army in the 1990s and I'd tried to get some money out of the cashpoint but my PIN number wasn't recognised. So I got back in my car and as I was driving off, looked over at the cashpoint which was beeping like mad, and £200 was hanging out. There was no one around; if there had have been, I would have seen them.

Some years after I left the army, I was driving along an A road one day and saw two fire engines and a police car in a field alongside it where a car had come off the road. A woman was still trapped inside it. I could see that it was a really difficult operation so I stopped and offered to help, giving the emergency workers instructions which led to us freeing her. Sadly, I learnt later that she didn't survive.

Before this happened, I'd written down a wish list of fishing gear I wanted to get. There were some specific, niche, items on the list. About a week after the accident, I was on eBay looking for the items and a guy got in touch and said he thought he had the items I was looking for. He only lived twenty minutes down the road so we met in a pub car park and he opened up the boot of his car and he had everything on my list, almost exactly. I honestly think it was the lady's way of thanking me for trying to help her.

My family have also experienced weird stuff. My wife has felt hands around her neck in the night as if trying to strangle her. She also fell backwards off a little step in the garden and felt hands on her back pushing her back up. And she's felt someone tickling her feet while she's been lying in bed.

And when my son was in his early twenties, he saw the light in his room start swinging all of a sudden. He filmed it on his phone. And he said when he kicked his slippers off, on a couple of occasions, after they landed, they flipped over to the right way up.

One of the craziest experiences I've ever had was when I was driving home on my birthday, December 14th, one year in my thirties. The car radio kept going on and off intermittently, so I tried to connect my phone to the radio instead, but that didn't work either, so I just thought, I'm done with this, and turned it off.

Then all of a sudden, the radio came on and blared out, 'Happy Birthday' by Altered Images, and then went off again! I laughed my head off all the way home.

Other random stuff has happened, like a psychic in pub once told me, 'Get that tattoo removed from your arm'. The tattoo was the name of an ex-girlfriend who I broke up with after finding out she'd cheated on me lots of times.

And, one Christmas I went to get these big scissors with orange handles from the middle drawer in the kitchen where they were always kept, to wrap the presents. All my family said they hadn't moved them, but we looked all over for them just in case, but couldn't find them. The next day, my sister opened the drawer and there they were. Our nan, who was in spirit, had been a dressmaker all her life, and we think she was playing a game with us!

After I left the army I worked collecting the bins for a bit and one day I was talking to the driver and told him I had a thing for redheads. We carried on with our rounds and at about 8.10am we pulled into a pub car park to do their bins and a woman with red hair was sitting there in a red convertible. She got out and beckoned me over and gave me a card which just said, 'Lisa' on it. She said, 'If you ever want to get away, let me know.' I put it in my pocket but when I went to retrieve it later it had gone. I honestly think she was some sort of angel. But I never did work out what the purpose or message was, if there was one.

BECKY

When I was in my twenties I started meditating and seeing spirits in my mind's eye. Often I'd meditate after work, sometimes for hours. When I came out of it I'd feel really awake and energised. I got really addicted to it! On one of the first occasions, I saw a huge eye, my mind's eye, opening up. It was like a kaleidoscope spinning round. That's how it started.

Soon after that, when I was meditating I saw a man lying on a hospital bed. I felt like his spirit was trapped in his body. And then I saw a tunnel of light and instinctively told him to go through the tunnel. It suddenly brightened up as he went through it, and then closed behind him. Another medium told me I'd done a 'soul rescue', when a person needs help going over to the Other Side.

This happened a lot from then on. Every time I closed my eyes and meditated I had people coming to me for help passing over. It was like they came to me because they were stuck between worlds. Another time, years after a teenage girl in my town was murdered, she came through to me when I was meditating and I saw a red car and a number of a B road which led out of town to a nearby village. Another time, she drew a map in my mind's eye which I then drew on bits of paper. It was like she'd taken over my hand and was drawing for me. When the line went off the page I'd get another bit of paper and carry on drawing, so in the end the map was on several bits of paper. I left them with my sister who stuck them together. The girl had put a cross on the map too of where her body was. Me and my sister went to find her body but never did. I think my sister must have stuck the pieces of paper together in the wrong order.

When we were there looking for her, we both saw something like a transparent bird fly past us. And later I saw lights, like fairy lights by the window of my mum's house, and sensed it was her. The girl would always come to me when I was meditating at my mum's house for some reason. One time I felt like I was her, lying there, stiff and cold, like she was buried. Her body was never discovered.

Often I'd be lying there meditating and there would be a line of spirits waiting for me to help them pass over. I would just say to them, 'Go to the light', and they would. Other times, I'd be lying there and people would come really close to me, right in my face and wave at me. I was finding it quite draining at this point so would try and ignore them!

One time, I was doing a guided meditation through an app on my phone and the alarm went off, but I hadn't set the alarm. I was a bit bored of that meditation anyway so I switched to another guided meditation without reading what it was about. I saw my dog and my nan, who had both passed away, and I saw myself cuddled up to a baby I believed to be the child I lost when I was younger; babies who are aborted or miscarried carry on growing up in spirit. I felt like my nan was looking after her in spirit. When I stopped I saw that the meditation was entitled, *'Meet your loved ones in Spirit'*.

When I was doing Reiki on a lady once, I got a vison of a rainbow and was overcome with sadness. Afterwards, she said her dad had died a few days ago and on the day he'd died, she'd seen a beautiful rainbow and showed me the photo she'd taken of it.

When I did a group meditation for world peace once, I had this beautiful vision of hundreds and hundreds of people holding hands in a massive circle.

I stopped meditating because it got a bit tiring; every time I closed my eyes I'd be visited! And, I had no one to talk to about it; everyone I did talk to said it wasn't real and it was my imagination. So I deliberately closed my third eye.

STEPH

I moved to Exeter with my husband and daughter in 2015 and we lived in a large Georgian house. I always felt a sense of doom on the landing at the top of the stairs, and on the stairs. One day, I went into my daughter's room and saw the figure of a little boy in the window, like he was stood in front of it. It was a dark figure so I couldn't make out his features. I went out and came back in again and it was gone.

I didn't mention any of this to my husband until we moved out a few months later, when he told me that he had had the sense that he was going to be pushed down the stairs when he was at the top of them.

Our next house was a 17th century Devon longhouse which had been a cider farm, in the village of Tedburn St Mary near Exeter. It was a huge house with thick white walls. And it had a really bad vibe. I would do yoga sometimes in the lounge and every time, I'd feel a cold breath on my face to the point I couldn't do it anymore.

My friend, who was a bit psychic, visited me from Croydon, where I'd lived before Devon, and one day we were sat chatting in my lounge. I was facing out towards the window, from which you could see for miles, and my friend was facing into the room, when suddenly she jerked her head and her eyes as if she'd seen something in the room. I asked her what she'd seen but she said nothing; she knew I was a wuss so didn't want to scare me.

When we were upstairs later, she stopped and stared at something again, and this time told me it was a little girl, she same one she'd seen downstairs running across the living room earlier. She said she was wearing a white dress and pigtails, but didn't get a sense of foreboding or anything.

LESLEY

I was brought up in a home where religion wasn't important; my family didn't have strong beliefs, but, growing up, I went to church a few times. My granddad died when I was six. He was hugely important to me, and when he died I always had this feeling of him being around me, but I never told anyone.

I used to play imaginary games as a youngster and one of them was being part of a quiz show like *University Challenge*. My three teammates were members of my family who had died. I thought it was a game, but I was really communicating with them. It was much later when I found out it's just as common to see spirit in your mind's eye, as it is in front of you. Later on, I started seeing spirits in front of me.

I was in my mid-teens when I went through a period where I'd think things and say things that would come true, for example, I once said, 'So and so is going to have a car accident soon if they carry on driving like that,' and then two days later they had a car accident. They were premonitions, but I didn't know they were premonitions. After I foresaw three people having accidents in separate incidents, which all ended up happening, I closed down. It scared me because I worried that I'd caused it.

Around that time, my mum had got more into spiritualism and became a healer. We started to see gemstones come into our family, either as gifts or we'd buy them. I was never interested in healing at that point, because I was always very scientifically minded, so unless I saw the evidence, I didn't believe something.

A long time later, when I was about thirty, my nan died. In the house every night between when she died and when she was buried, a ceiling light went on. The first time it happened I thought my husband had done it. Then I thought it was the kids, but they weren't physically strong enough to switch it on because you had to press the button quite firmly. So I said, 'If it's you, Nan, do it tomorrow night.' That night, a different light, a lamp, switched on. We knew it was her, then.

My mum bought me an astrology reading and the reader said I was clairsentient. To me, I just thought I had good intuition. I went home and looked up clairsentience and then bought a set of Tarot cards.

Two years later, my mum had three friends over from the spiritualist church for coffee. When I was sitting with them, a male friend of one of the mediums, who was in spirit, came through to me. What happened to him came out of my mouth before I could stop it. He had gone up on Clifton Suspension Bridge in Bristol and jumped off, his coat was full of stones. His friend cried because she'd never told anyone how he died.

That experience taught me to be careful about what to say, because some people don't want to hear. It was a pivotal moment in my development.

Sometime later, I was on a course and working with a man I didn't know. We were sat quietly one evening and I saw myself in my mind's eye, falling from a height. I felt this was a message for him and found myself saying, 'Zoom, zoom' out loud, while hearing helicopter blades. I told him I got the feeling a helicopter was falling out of the sky. I thought it was so weird, but he told me to continue because he recognised the information. 'Please don't stop', he said. I starting feeling like I was actually falling.

I told him that in the helicopter crash three out of four people died. Then I started hearing the song *Virginia Plain* by *Roxy Music* in my mind's ear, on repeat. The information was being repeated until I put it into words and he validated it. The crash happened in Virginia Water in Surrey. The man who died wanted to get a message to his wife; his wife was the man's sister.

I said it was an interesting funeral because there was a man in a wheelchair, one of the survivors, sitting next to a woman in a bright yellow hat. That was what his sister used to wear. I just thought, gosh this is freaky, let's quit now!

I have earthbound spirits who come to me needing help going over. I used to pass an accident spot on a main road, and a man was stood there all the time. One time, when I was a passenger in a car driving past, I spoke to him telepathically, and told him he needed to go over and he shouldn't be stood there. I asked him, 'Why are you there? Standing looking at your dead body isn't a nice way to be.' He replied, 'I don't know what to do.' I didn't know anything about sending people over at the time so I looked it up on Google and the next time I went past I said, 'Go to the light.' It looked very dark around him, and the accident had happened in the dark. I nagged him to, 'look at the light.' I showed him where the light was and telepathically pushed him towards it. And then he went, and I never saw him again.

I went on to develop reading the Tarot. When I was a single mum, one evening I felt exhausted and just wanted to be on my own and get an early night, but I had this nagging feeling that I had to invite my friend over. She came over straight from work at 5.30pm and she opened up to me about how things had been really difficult with her boyfriend. We had glass of wine and a chat and she went home.

In the morning, I got a phone call from her employer informing me that her boyfriend had taken his own life the night before. When I got to her, she was in a terrible state and showed me the letter he'd left her saying, 'I don't know where the hell you are, but we were supposed to go together, so I've gone on my own.' It read like he was planning on taking her life too. When I was driving home from work the next day, something was hitting the roof of my car over and over again, about twenty times. It was him, cross at me for stopping her from coming home.

When this sort of thing happens, you realise being a medium is not a little thing, but huge. I take it so seriously. I've been out with my friends and they've wanted to do the Tarot cards, but I've told them, 'No, it's so serious.' And I would never ever do a Ouija board.

A friend became ill with COVID-19, but she thought it was the flu. Her mum and dad came through to me and told me their daughter had the virus. Three months later, she was still no better and one particular day when she felt really poorly, her parents came through to me again and told me to tell her to go to hospital now, that day. She didn't go, but rang the doctor who told her to take paracetamol. She collapsed a few hours later. She was taken to hospital in an ambulance and ended up losing half her lung function. They were adamant about her going to hospital to prevent her lung collapsing. Her dead mum and dad diagnosed something the NHS didn't!

In my thirties I became a higher education lecturer, which I did for twenty years before ill health meant I stopped and started reading full time. During this time, I'd get messages for my fellow teachers, some of which were really well received and others which really upset people. It taught me to only give a reading for someone who asks for one.

I had a client who lived up north. She showed me some photos and I picked up that one was of her mother in spirit, but for some reason I just couldn't see her as her mother. When I said this to her, she told me it was her adopted mother. The message I got for her, was, 'If you ever go and see your biological family, you must take someone with you because you'll find out something that will be extremely upsetting.'

She decided to visit her 'real' family in Ireland. But despite my warning, went on her own. Once there, they told her that her birth mother and her auntie had both died of breast cancer. She had to undertake the long journey back, by boat and car, with this devasting news, all by herself. Once home, she requested a test which found that she already had breast cancer. She had to have a double mastectomy.

I've given messages to women and told them to leave their partners because they'll be violent. They've stayed with them anyway and then come back to me with their faces covered in bruises.

I've read a lot for people's pets, some of which are alive and some which have passed over. Often, if the animals are alive, their owners ask for readings because they're adopted or have emotional problems and people want to know they're doing enough for them.

My husband became worried about me. He too realised that mediumship is not all rosy and is something to be taken extremely seriously. If you have the gift, it can sometimes feel like it's not a gift; you have to accept the realisation that you need to pass messages on for as long as they want you to and work in a way that's joyous and fantastic but also bizarre, weird and tiring. It takes massive concentration to tune in, and often you're talking to three people at once; the person you're giving the reading to in real life, the person or people in spirit, and your guide to help you interpret the messages.

I found that the more I experienced and the better I became, the more detailed the messages became, but also the more tiring it became. You have to be as healthy as you can be. I have to sleep well, eat well and organise my life well in order to give readings most days. And I don't drink alcohol at all because it affects me the next day, and that's not fair on the person I'm reading for. So I live a fairly restricted life.

I know mediums who have been retired by spirit; they simply become unable to channel messages anymore. This is usually because they've become lax in preparing themselves or protecting themselves.

As I developed, my guides changed. My grandad is there as my gatekeeper. Then I had a guide from Africa who rocked up many years ago; I used to ask him the questions, but now I just get the information when I need it.

I've never wanted publicity. I've been asked for interviews and TV work but turned them down. I worked the 'psychic lines' (telephone) for six months and then, when I stopped, my clients went out of their way to find me.

Giving someone a reading is a form of education, helping them with their game plan and helping them follow a direction which would be good for them and which they hadn't thought about before. I know my guide is intrinsically there. I open up at the beginning of the day and close down at the end. And before every reading, I ask for them, and say thank you to them at the end.

I'd much rather do readings where I'm not looking into the future for people because what you see is what it's like on that day, and whether it happens or not is down to so many factors; it's all down to your choices and other people's choices as to whether you get to that point or not. There are too many variables, one little thing can knock you off that path and you may never find your way back to it.

There isn't a defined path for us, when you get to each crossroads, which direction do you go? That's entirely down to you, and no one can foresee that.

GLOSSARY

CHAKRAS – Energy centres in the human body. First referred to in Hinduism's oldest sacred texts, the Vedas, there are seven chakras which run from the top of the head down the spine. Chakra is a Sanskrit word and means 'wheel'. These wheels of energy correspond with specific organs and affect our physical as well as our emotional well-being, so keeping them 'open' and healthy is important.

CLAIRALIENCE – Clear smelling; awareness of paranormal activity through scent.

CLAIRAUDIENCE – Clear hearing; awareness of paranormal activity, either with your real ears or your mind's ear.

CLAIRCOGNISANCE – Clear knowing; a sense of knowing, either through your higher self or your spirit guide.

CLAIRGUSTANCE – Clear smelling; awareness of paranormal activity through taste.

CLAIRSENTIENCE – Clear feeling; perceiving emotional or psychic energy that is imperceptible to the other five senses.

CLAIRVOYANCE – Clear seeing; awareness of paranormal activity, either with your real eyes or your mind's eye.

DIVINATION – The practice of seeking knowledge about the future by supernatural means, such as Oracle cards or dowsing rods.

DOWSING – Forked or Y-shaped wood or metal rods used to pick up on energetic vibrations and locate water or other minerals. Also called divining rods.

EGO – The less conscious, less spiritually connected part of the human psyche, linked with our personality, which is more aligned with less meaningful pursuits.

EMPATH – Someone who feels above average empathy.

FIRST NATIONS – Canada's indigenous people (in addition to Métis and Inuit).

HIGHER SELF – Your real essence; your conscious spiritual self, separate from your personality and unencumbered by the ego.

INTUITION – Understanding at an instinctive level without the need for conscious reasoning.

KARMA – A central belief in Buddhism and Hinduism, the law of cause and effect; there are consequences for our actions.

Law of Attraction – A philosophy that positive thoughts attract positive experiences and negative thoughts attract negative experiences.

Ley lines – Invisible energy pathways believed to carry a powerful magnetic field, or psychic power, linking or aligning ancient, prominent or sacred landmarks.

Lightworkers – People who serve others and the planet; part of their life purpose is to instigate positive change.

Manifesting – To bring something into reality through purposeful thoughts.

Medium – Someone able to communicate with the spirit world.

Mind's ear – Hearing paranormal phenomenon with your inner ear.

Mind's eye – Seeing paranormal phenomenon with your inner eye. Also known as your 'third eye'.

Native Americans – The United States of America's indigenous people.

Oracle cards – A deck of cards, including Tarot and Angel cards, used to connect with the spirit world and believed to be influenced by the spirit world.

Orbs – Energy of spirits manifesting as balls of light. Also, telepathically created balls of light energy.

Psychic – Someone able to receive and perceive supernatural information beyond what our five senses are capable of.

Psychometry – Extrasensory perception and knowledge about something or someone through connecting with it on a psychic level.

Psychopomp – Soul clearing; helping earthbound souls move on to the Other Side.

Reiki – A form of spiritual healing which draws upon the energy within us and around us, and from God/source energy.

Samsara – A central belief of Buddhism and Hinduism, the cycle of life and death, indefinite rebirths due to karma.

Schumann resonances – Electromagnetic peaks in the Earth's low frequency.

Scrying – Using a reflective object or fire to foresee the future.

Sixth sense – Intuition or extrasensory perception; awareness of information not perceived by the other physical senses.

Somatics – The relationship of the physical body and the mind.

SPIRIT GUIDE – A human in spirit who has chosen to be your discarnate guide throughout your life.

SPIRIT GUARD – A human in spirit who has chosen to protect you from negative supernatural influences.

SPIRITUAL HEALING – The method of healing through channelling the healing energy of God/source energy, or the spirit world.

STAR CHILD – A psychic child whose life purpose is to bring about positive change.

SUPERNATURAL/PARANORMAL – Phenomena beyond the scientific laws of nature.

THIRD EYE – Seeing paranormal phenomenon with your inner eye. Also known as your 'mind's eye'.

RECOMMENDED READING

Ask and it is Given, Esther and Jerry Hicks, Hay House, 2005

Never say Goodbye, Patrick Matthews, Llewellyn Publications, 2003

The Power of Now, Eckhart Tolle, Yellow Kite, 2001

Spiritual Growth, Sanaya Roman, H J Kramer, 1988

Women Who Run with the Wolves: Myths and Stories of the Wild Woman Archetype, Clarissa Pinkola Estés, Ballantine Books, 1992

ACKNOWLEDGEMENTS

Thank you to my brother Adam and my sister-in-law Helen for keeping me on the straight and narrow, not an easy task! Thank you to Bex, Nic and Marina, whose experiences contained within these pages are nothing short of magical. And thank you to Amy, Helena, Linda, Steph, Dan, Becky and Lesley for sharing your experiences as part of this work, which further helped me fulfil my aim of providing a balanced presentation of the spirit world. Thank you to Sam at Swatt Books, for steering me adeptly through the self-publishing process. Thank you Mum and Dad for always supporting me. Thank you Mike, for being the best dad to our wonderfully exuberant boy. Thank you to my guide Quentin and all my loved ones in spirit, including my four grandparents. And thank you Woody, for exuding light and bringing joy to all those who are lucky enough to meet you. Finally, thank you, Jean.

AUTHOR'S NOTE

The main experiences are presented as my own, but on whole, belong to someone else, close to me, for whom I am honouring their wish for anonymity. Several other people have generously shared their truths for the story, which have immeasurably helped me fulfil my objective of presenting as broad an insight into the spirit world as I possibly could, and to whom I am so grateful. Unless specified in the text, references to geopolitical and climate change events, including facts, figures and quotes – namely, in the Humans v Mother Nature chapter – have been widely reported, often by multiple, online news outlets. In the rare event that the original news source(s) are deleted from the World Wide Web in the future, rendering the information in the text being untraceable and therefore unverifiable, the information as reported was accurate at the time of publication in September 2025. The views expressed in the story are my own, and no offence is meant towards those holding alternative views. I have endeavoured to show the utmost respect for the First Nations people of Canada when mentioning their spirituality and their plight in society over the years.

ABOUT THE AUTHOR

Fran grew up in Exmouth, Devon, UK, and studied Religious Studies at Cardiff University, graduating with a 2:1 in 2003 after which she moved to her 'spiritual home', the mountains of British Colombia, Canada, living there until 2005. In her mid-20s she 'found' writing, becoming a journalist in 2009. Her *raison d'être* became giving people a voice and holding authority to account. With a background in fine art, Fran taught herself how to wield a digital camera on maternity leave, with photography quickly becoming an important creative outlet, passion and side hustle. She is a doting mother to her son Woody, a bright spark who emanates joy wherever he goes. Fran wrote this book while juggling single motherhood and running her own business.

www.ingramcontent.com/pod-product-compliance
Lightning Source LLC
Chambersburg PA
CBHW010248010526
44119CB00055B/774